CONGREGATIONAL MEMBERS OF PARLIAMENT IN THE NINETEENTH CENTURY

David W. Bebbington

Professor Bebbington gave his lecture on *Congregational Members of Parliament in the Nineteenth Century* at Westminster College, Cambridge on 23 September 2006, the occasion being the Annual Lecture of the United Reformed Church History Society.

CONGREGRATIONAL MEMBERS OF PARLIAMENT IN THE NINETEENTH CENTURY

David W. Bebbington

Occasional Publication No 1

The United Reformed Church History Society
The Congregational History Society

2007

ISBN-10 0-8-5346-261-5
ISBN-13 978-0-85346-261-3

EAN 9780853462613

In November 1879, the month when Gladstone launched a scathing denunciation of the existing Conservative government in his Midlothian speeches, it was clear that a general election would soon be upon the country. Accordingly the Liberal electors of Ashton-under-Lyne assembled in their Town Hall to choose a prospective parliamentary candidate. It had been arranged that H. M. Bompas, a London lawyer and a Congregationalist, should be brought forward for adoption. The chair was taken by Hugh Mason, a cotton master of the town and another Congregationalist, but soon matters began to go awry. Instead of proceeding to select Bompas as the party managers had planned, the audience began to display a decided preference for Mason, the local man, demanding that he should agree on the spot to be the candidate. "Don't let him go", they cried, "until he promises!" Mason was intensely popular in the town, especially with his own workpeople, for whom he had introduced a Saturday half-holiday in the teeth of opposition from his fellow-employers. It was said that on Sundays he was cheered in the street as he made his way to chapel. Seeing how strongly people felt, Bompas decided to give way and threw his support behind the Ashton manufacturer.[1] Bompas was never to enter parliament, but Mason duly carried the Ashton seat in April 1880 and so crowned a career of public service to his native town by representing it in the House of Commons. It is a vivid instance of the way in which nineteenth-century Congregational MPs were normally rooted in particular communities. With relatively few exceptions, they were the champions of their home towns rather than professional politicians.[2]

This study attempts to scrutinise this whole set of local heroes, the Congregationalists elected to the House of Commons during the nineteenth century, in their specific settings. The period extends from before the first Reform Act, for the first Congregational MP of the century, John Wilks, was elected in 1830, down to 1900, for those returned in the Khaki election of that year have been included. The oldest, Edward Baines senior, was born in 1774; the last to be alive, T. C. Taylor, died as recently as 1952. Defining who is a Congregational MP is a knotty issue. Many figures hover on the borderline. Several who were thought at the time to be Congregationalists turn out not to have been so. Thus D. A. Thomas, eventually Viscount Rhondda, attended Tabernacle English Congregational Church, Aberdare, as a boy, became an agnostic at university, was baptised as an Anglican at twenty-six and in later years, according to his daughter, did not know how much he believed.[3] A few had abandoned an impeccable Congregational background. As Clyde Binfield, to whom this paper is greatly indebted, has shown, H. H. Asquith, whose family was steeped in northern Independency, who at fifteen had joined St Leonard's on Sea Congregational Church and who as an attender signed R. F. Horton's invitation to Hampstead in 1883, had allowed his religious allegiance to be extinguished.[4] In other cases there is insufficient evidence to be sure that a certain MP was a Congregational church member. John Frederick Cheetham, for example, the son of another MP who was an undoubted Congregationalist, is associated by the historian of Lancashire Congregationalism with the Stalybridge church, but not actually said to have been a member.[5] The problem commonly arises, as in this instance, where the family's allegiance is plain but the individual's less so. There are also uniquely problematic figures. Sir Culling Eardley Eardley, treasurer of the Hertfordshire Union of Independents and Baptists and of the London Missionary Society, favoured Congregational principles but worshipped as an Evangelical Anglican. James Allanson Picton served in the Congregational ministry before he entered parliament, but by then he was well on the path to Spinozan pantheism. Henry James Wilson was nurtured in the denomination and sometimes attended Sheffield Congregational churches, but when asked why he was not in chapel more often he replied, "I so often want to move an amendment to the sermon."[6] Most of these marginal figures have been reluctantly excluded from the analysis, but it incorporates a small number who are likely to have been church members but for whom absolutely compelling evidence is lacking.[7] One man who was not in membership when he was an MP has been included: Sir Titus Salt, who did not make a public profession of faith until later in the year he left the Commons, but who had already founded a Congregational church in his model village of Saltaire.[8] Two, Keir Hardie and John Wilson, were technically in the Evangelical Union, but since this sister denomination in Scotland merged with Congregationalism in 1896, they have been deemed to qualify. The total number of MPs in the resulting analysis is one hundred and two, though if other possible candidates were confirmed, the figure might increase by around a dozen. It is a substantial number, especially when compared to the equivalent Baptist total, which was only nineteen.[9] It is a reminder that Congregationalists were by no means averse to public life during the reign of Victoria.

We can begin by examining the occupations of the group. Fourteen, including Hugh Mason, were cotton masters, and the same number were in other textiles: five in woollens, five in worsted and one each in linen, alpaca, silk and card clothing. One was in the associated trade of dyeing and another in hosiery. Twenty-three were in other types of manufacturing: carpets, earthenware, soap, sugar, tinplate, iron, steel, machinery, wagons, bricks, tobacco and so on. Three were in coal mining and two at gas works. Ten were merchants or carriers in widely varied fields such as timber, coal, paper and animal skins. Trade and industry were therefore overwhelmingly predominant, occupying fully two-thirds of the MPs. Some of them were hugely successful entrepreneurs: Sir Frank Crossley owned the largest carpet factory in the world at Dean Clough Mills, Halifax; Joseph Ruston of Lincoln, with the motto "My customer is my best friend", employed over 2,500 people, supplied seventy excavators for the Manchester Ship Canal and opened a branch in Budapest; John Remington Mills and Samuel Morley became millionaires. Many of these men also participated in related financial fields, several of them founding or joining the board of banks. There was in addition one specialist banker and one building society promoter (a scoundrel). Two were publishers and ten were newspaper proprietors, the large number being partly explained by the closeness of the newspapers to the political world. The professional subgroup was dominated by the lawyers, of whom there were sixteen. Several of their number had interests in the commercial, manufacturing or transport sectors: one, George Leeman of York, was more of a railway magnate than a solicitor. There were four who began as ministers, one of them unordained, but who turned into businessmen (William Shaw and Halley Stewart) or else political activists (Edward Miall and Henry Richard). The one other individual who might be counted as a professional was one of the gasworks proprietors who began as a civil engineer. There was only a single farmer amongst them. The group was therefore preponderantly a reflection of the dawning industrial age: men who were thrusting, successful and prosperous.

The Congregational MPs, then, were most obviously representatives of the new urban civilisation celebrated in a work published in 1842, *The Age of Great Cities*. The book was an analysis of the place of Victorian Britain in the sweep of world events by Robert Vaughan, the first professor of modern history at University College, London, and from 1843 the principal of the Lancashire Independent College. In the contemporary "struggle between the feudal and the civic" sketched by Vaughan there was no doubt that the great majority of the Congregational MPs were drawn from what he called "the mercantile class" and none belonged naturally to "the landlord class".[10] Many – at least ten – were active in Chambers of Commerce. One of them, Henry Ripley of Bradford, was in 1859 the first president of the executive of the Association of Chambers of Commerce, and in 1909 another, Albert Spicer, became president of the Chambers of Commerce of the Empire at Sydney. A significant proportion of them, no fewer than eleven, were strong advocates of the reform of the land laws so that the countryside should not prosper at the expense of the cities. Yet we should not too readily stereotype this body of men as urban warriors hostile to the reactionary influences of the open fields. Many of them acquired homes outside the towns where they made their money. Thus Thomas Shaw, a Halifax woollen manufacturer, bought a home in Stainland, a place three and a half miles away. The men whose firms thrived most, such as Frank Crossley, Remington Mills and Samuel Morley, turned themselves into country squires. Apsley Pellatt, a Southwark glass manufacturer, retired to Staines in Middlesex, where he established a model farm; J. J. Colman, the Norwich mustard manufacturer, became a breeder of red polled cattle on his estate near Lowestoft, the herd selling on his death for 4,262$1/2$ guineas. There is a sense in which many of the Congregational MPs aspired to a place in the traditional feudal order. They were not, at any rate, a solid group of its inveterate opponents.

Nor were the representatives of Congregationalism in parliament merely thoughtless capitalists who exploited their workers. There was, it is true, industrial tension in some of their undertakings. Titus Salt would not consider allowing trade union organisation in his factory. Joseph Ruston at Lincoln peremptorily refused the demand of his workmen for increased wages with the remark, "I hope you will let me get bread and cheese out of my business", and ever afterwards was known as "bread and cheese".[11] Many of these strong-minded individuals could be angular in their dealings with subordinates. Even a sympathetic obituary notice of William Crosfield, a Liverpool sugar boiler, admitted that he was "of a choleric temperament".[12] Yet what was far more noticeable about the normal attitude of these businessmen to their employees was a solicitude for their wellbeing verging on paternalism. Robert Milligan, a Bradford worsted manufacturer, gave an annual feast to his workers; Benjamin Whitworth, a cotton master, built institutes for his employees at Fleetwood in Lancashire and Drogheda in Ireland; and Colman provided a wide range of welfare facilities. Salt, Mason and Ripley were celebrated for the model villages they erected for the families that depended on them. A form of profit sharing was introduced by Frank Crossley as early as 1864, and subsequently by Thomas Barnes, a Bolton cotton manufacturer, and by T. C. Taylor, a Batley woollen manufacturer who became the apostle of the idea.[13] Morley actively supported the growth of trade unionism, financing the National Agricultural Trade Labourers' Union, and two of the MPs, Samuel Plimsoll and Batty Langley, acted as presidents of trade unions, for seamen and railway clerks respectively. Edward Miall, the founder of the Anti-State Church Society, was also one of the earliest advocates of employment exchanges. In 1892-93, under Congregational Union auspices, there were two consultations between MPs representing the Labour interest and those representing the denomination, yielding a statement of the paramountcy of right over expediency in industrial disputes.[14] Walter McLaren, a Keighley worsted spinner, was known for supporting industrial conciliation, and J. H. Whitley, a Halifax cotton spinner and later Speaker of the Commons, chaired a wartime committee that created the Whitley Councils to harmonise the relations of employers and employees. These men were no Gradgrinds. They were generally eager, not least in their own interest, to promote the contentment of the working people.

What, then, of their politics? The MPs, as might be expected, were over-whelmingly Liberal. They supported the party at once associated, at least in part, with the advance of urban/industrial values and with the defence of civil and religious liberties. Evan Richards, a Swansea steel manufacturer, was typical in expressing, as he did in 1873, his confidence in "the wisdom and integrity of Mr. Gladstone".[15] Many of the MPs were leading figures in local Liberal affairs. Thus Edward Holden, a Walsall currier, became chairman of the town's Liberal Association and Batty Langley, a timber merchant, was president of its Sheffield counterpart. Hugh Mason arranged that the National Liberal Federation, the organisation created by Joseph Chamberlain to link the various local bodies, should meet at Ashton in 1882. A few of the Congregationalists in parliament were on the moderate wing of the party. In particular, Adam Black, the founder of the Edinburgh publishers Adam and

Charles Black, was more of a Whig than a Liberal, supporting T. B. Macaulay as the town's MP between 1839 and 1847, opposing local radicals and actually voting against parliamentary reform in the 1860s. Later on there were others who looked askance at the pace of change. In 1898 Thomas Wayman, a retired Halifax wool merchant, while, like most Liberals, endorsing the reform of the House of Lords, also described himself in *Dod's Parliamentary Companion* as favouring the maintenance of the constitution.[16] A larger proportion of the Congregationalists, however, belonged over the years to the radical tendencies in the party. Titus Salt chaired an Anti-Corn Law meeting in 1842 that endorsed the six points of the People's Charter; and Thomas Leuty, a Leeds linen manufacturer, was one of several who in the later years of the century supported the advanced Newcastle Programme and even the limitation of miners' work to eight hours. One, famously, broke with the Liberal Party altogether to take separate political action on behalf of the working people. This was James Keir Hardie, the former Scottish miner, who was a member of Cumnock Evangelical Union Church when he became Independent Labour candidate for mid-Lanark in 1888, the prelude to the establishment of the Independent Labour Party and eventually of the Labour Representation Committee in 1900. The great majority of the other Congregationalists, however, were content with some variant of Liberalism.

The exceptions are particularly instructive. There were two MPs among the Congregationalists elected as Conservatives. Edward Ball, MP for Cambridge-shire from 1852 to 1863, was a member of Burwell Congregational Church, where the balls on the parapet are supposed to bear architectural witness to the influence of his family in chapel affairs. His Conservatism, which entailed endorsement of the established church, must have been primarily a conse-quence of his occupation as a farmer. He was one of those who feared the consequences of free trade for British agriculture so much that they threw in their lot with the Protectionism professed by the Conservatives under Lord Derby. The other member of the party, Richard Pilkington, MP for the Newton division of Lancashire from 1899 to 1905, was a partner in the family glass-making firm at St Helens and a deacon at Ormskirk Street Congregational Church in the town. Coming from a place where the Protestant/Catholic divide eclipsed the rivalry between church and chapel, Pilkington seems to have embraced the Conservatives as the natural defenders of Protestantism. There were also five Congregational MPs who joined the Liberal Unionists, the section of the party that seceded in opposition to Gladstone's Home Rule proposals for Ireland in 1886. One of them, Benjamin Whitworth, had ceased to sit in the Commons before the Home Rule split; another, Joseph Ruston, declined to stand in 1886 because of his aversion to Gladstone's proposal. Two of the three who served as Liberal Unionist MPs, William Caine and John Jones-Jenkins, eventually returned to the Liberals. Only Thomas Lea, a Kidderminster ironfounder who had previously sat for County Donegal, remained a staunch Liberal Unionist. He was the sole Congregational Unionist to stand at the 1892 general election.[17] Jones-Jenkins, a Swansea tinplate manufacturer, is of further interest because his political trajectory from Liberalism to Liberal Unionism was paralleled by a religious shift, first from a Welsh-speaking Independent chapel to the more prestigious English-speaking Walter Road Congregational Church, Swansea, and then to the Church of England.[18] Another who had travelled a similar road a few years before was Henry Ripley, a Bradford dyer, who was returned for the town as a Liberal in 1868, but who stood in 1874 as a Liberal Conservative and by 1880 styled himself a Moderate Conservative. There was a simultaneous religious evolution, from Horton Lane Congregational Chapel, where in 1861 he laid the foundation stone of the new building, to occasional Anglican attendance around 1870 and to outright support for the Bradford Church Institute by 1876.[19] Thus Conservatism, together with Liberal Unionism, was rare among Congregationalists. The last two cases, furthermore, illustrate the extent to which Dissent and Liberalism formed part of a single package. When one melted away, the other might also dissolve.

There was a further political allegiance that claimed two of the MPs. William Shaw and William Abraham were both Irish Home Rulers. Shaw, who had served as an Independent minister in Cork, had been connected with the quixotic nationalism of Young Ireland in the 1840s, and, after turning into a businessman, presided in 1873 at the conference that established the first Home Rule League. In 1879 Shaw was elected leader of the Home Rule Party. He lasted only a year in office, being ousted by Charles Stewart Parnell as the movement turned radical in the wake of the land agitation. In 1885 his fortunes collapsed at the failure of the Munster Bank, of which he was chairman, but in politics he had earned himself the soubriquet "Sensible Shaw". He was the only nineteenth-century Congregationalist to have led a United Kingdom political party. Abraham, a Limerick man who entered parliament in 1885, was also prominent in Home Rule affairs, becoming joint treasurer of the party. Although he remained in parliament down to his death in 1915, his moment of celebrity came in 1890, when he proposed the resolution removing Parnell from the leadership of the party, so precipitating the long-term division among the Home Rulers. There were muted echoes of Irish nationalism among the four Congregationalists holding Scottish seats (there were five expatriate Scots in English seats) and the seven representing Wales. John Wilson, a Glasgow iron tube manufacturer, thought that if Ireland received Home Rule, Scotland deserved it too; and John Leng, editor of the *Dundee Advertiser,* wrote a book entitled *Home Rule All Round* (1890). Welsh Nonconformist MPs tended to cast themselves in the role of champions of their small nation, and all three returned in 1868 were Congregationalists.[20] One of them, Henry Richard, had publicly defended the reputation of his homeland as long ago as 1847, and became known as "the Member for Wales". Later on the barrister David Brynmor Jones took up national issues, in 1910 becoming chairman of the Welsh Parliamentary Party. Unlike in Ireland, nationalism did not, in this period, draw Scottish or Welsh Congregational MPs away from their Liberal allegiance, but some of them did voice its claims.

What were the other issues to which the Congregational MPs gave their energies? Undoubtedly the prime cause was religious equality, the dismantling of the privileges of the established church. Traditionally the Dissenting Deputies had looked after the religious liberties of those outside the Church of England. During the period from 1844 to 1888, with the exception of only six years, the chairman of the Deputies was a Congregational MP: Remington Mills, Apsley Pellatt, Charles Reed and Henry Richard. Another, William Woodall, was briefly chairman at the end of the century. This body, however, was being superseded by more activist organisations. John Wilks, MP for Boston from 1830 to 1837, had founded, in 1811, the Protestant Society for the Protection of Religious Liberty for the defence of oppressed Dissenters. During the 1830s many of those who subsequently entered parliament were roused to political militancy by attempts to enforce the collection of church rates, which compelled Dissenters to support a form of worship with which they conscientiously disagreed. From the 1840s there was a new organisation, the Anti-State Church Association that from 1853 was called the Liberation Society, to press for the separation of church and state. Of the MPs, Edward Miall was its creator, Carvell Williams its chief administrator and Henry Richard one of its leading advocates. In 1871, Miall proposed and Richard seconded a Commons resolution in favour of English disestablishment; in 1885 Williams and Richard wrote the Society's standard handbook, *Disestablishment*. Many of the other MPs were glad to give their time to the society, with Halley Stewart still championing its cause long into the twentieth century. Nevertheless, some Congregationalists had their reservations. Samuel Morley resigned from the Liberation Society executive in 1868 because he no longer wished to put its sectional cause before the wider concerns of the Liberal Party. Another Congregational MP, John Dick Peddie, an Edinburgh architect, deliberately took Scottish disestablishment out of the hands of the Society in 1886 so that the campaign north of the border should not be held back by English preoccupations. By the end of the century, even though most Congregational MPs gave lip service to the disestablishment cause, it was no longer the priority it had once been.

A related issue was the education question. The tentative fostering of elementary schools for the people of England and Wales occupied a great deal of parliamentary time from 1833 onwards. Congregationalists knew that they did not want schools to be dominated by the Church of England. Several future MPs, including Charles Reed, a London typefounder, joined in the massive protest movement against the attempt in 1843 by Sir James Graham to create a system under the control of the Church of England. It was at that point that Edward Baines junior, co-editor of the *Leeds Mercury* and later MP for the city, invented educational voluntaryism, the doctrine that the state should have no more influence over popular education than over the church. From 1847 Henry Richard became secretary of the Voluntary School Association that tried to drum up Dissenting enthusiasm for the cause of schooling free from state interference. Baines, however, was to abandon voluntaryism in 1867, recognising that only state money could cope with the educational needs of the nation. From that point on, it became clear that Congregationalists were far from united about what they wanted. Reed, from 1868 an MP, from 1870 the vice-chairman of the London School Board and from 1873 its chairman, insisted that schools must teach the Bible. Others took the paradoxical line that the only way to preserve Christian teaching from state dilution was to exclude the Bible altogether from the schools. Several Congregational MPs, including Halley Stewart and Joseph Compton-Rickett, though profoundly religious men, became vociferous champions of this so-called secular solution. If religious equality tended to unite Congregational MPs, the issue of Bible or no Bible in schools deeply divided them. It was an indication that, even on questions with a religious flavour, they were no united phalanx in the Commons.

Beyond their commitments to disestablishment and education, the bulk of Congregationalists in parliament were notable for joining in the loudest cries of Victorian Liberalism, for peace, retrenchment and reform. Several participated in the organised movement to reduce armaments and encourage international arbitration. Henry Richard was secretary of the Peace Society from 1848 to 1885. Apsley Pellatt lost his seat in 1857 for voting against Lord Palmerston's bellicose ways. Hugh Mason deeply regretted being involved, as mayor of Ashton, in placing two Russian guns captured in the Crimea in front of the town hall. Yet not all the MPs were ill disposed towards matters military. Titus Salt, though believing in non-intervention abroad, also held that Britain should be able to defend herself and served as a colonel of Volunteers. At least five other MPs held some military or naval rank, and another gave a drill hall to the local Volunteers, though it is significant that half these men were among the handful of Conservatives and Unionists. The principle of retrenchment meant that the state must cut back on its expenditure and on its taxation alike. Eleven of the MPs once took part in the Anti-Corn Law League that championed free trade, with one, Thomas Shaw, a Halifax woollen manufacturer, serving as its honorary treasurer. Morley was prominent in the Administrative Reform Association that lobbied for reductions in the civil service; Frederick Doulton, the Lambeth earthenware manufacturer, favoured "the economical application of the public revenues"; and into the twentieth century, when free trade came under threat, it remained a favourite cause with several Congregational MPs such as Walter McLaren. Of all the secular causes, however, the favourite was parliamentary reform. The Baines, father and son, trumpeted the merits of the Great Reform Bill in the *Leeds Mercury*; in the 1850s Thomas Challis, a London skin broker, urged extension of the franchise, equal electoral districts and short parliaments; and Reed was one of many who urged the redistribution of seats in the prelude to the 1884 Reform Act. Only

Adam Black and George Leeman are known to have resisted proposals for broader parliamentary representation. The secret ballot in particular was a common demand in the years before it replaced, in 1872, the open hustings where men publicly declared their electoral choice. This change was not approved by Hugh Mason: the bluff Ashton manufacturer considered the secrecy of the ballot 'un-English'.[21] In general, however, there was widespread sympathy for the three linked ideals of promoting international harmony, reducing public waste and enlarging the electorate.

The MPs also increasingly demanded a range of social reforms. The most common was some form of temperance legislation. Benjamin Whitworth was chairman of the United Kingdom Alliance, the British prohibitionist organisation, from 1871 to 1891. So devoted was he to measures against alcohol that in 1872 he claimed "he would vote for the bluest Tory if only he were right on this question".[22] Mason and Caine were vice-presidents of the United Kingdom Alliance, with Caine also serving as president of the Congregational Total Abstinence Union. In 1881 Morley piloted through the Commons a bill banning the payment of wages in public houses. Like many other Nonconformist MPs, Mark Oldroyd, a Dewsbury woollen manufacturer, urged the right of communities to pass a local veto on alcohol. During the 1892 election, however, an observant opponent noticed that a wagon load of wines, spirits and beers was delivered to his home. Oldroyd excused himself rather lamely by saying that it was only a small load because "I drink it very slowly".[23] Other social causes claimed the support of a smaller number of the Congregationalists who sat in parliament. One, which was much more popular among Wesleyans, was the enforcement of Sunday rest. Pellatt gave evidence to a Commons select committee on the subject in 1832 and Reed opposed Sunday Post Office deliveries. T. C. Taylor was a persistent critic of British failure to suppress the opium trade. Like Taylor, Sir Joseph Leigh, a Stockport cotton manufacturer, was an early advocate of old age pensions. Several others, of whom Walter Hazell, a Leicester printer, was the chief, promoted social gospel solutions to the problems of the 1890s through agencies such as a training farm for the unemployed at Longley in Essex.[24] Social purity, a euphemism for the reduction of sexual immorality, was a concern of a few of the MPs including Crosfield and Morley. A cause that mobilised Congregationalists as much as the members of any other denomination, however, was the women's movement. It is true that Samuel Evans, a Welsh barrister, argued strenuously against female suffrage, but at least seven of the MPs were its advocates. Mason, though never endorsing the enfranchisement of wives, acted as leader of the women's suffrage group in the Commons from 1881 to 1884;[25] William Woodall, a Burslem potter, was chairman of the Central Committee for Women's Suffrage, proposing an amendment to the 1884 Reform Act and introducing women's suffrage bills in 1887, 1889 and 1891; and, before taking part in national organisations promoting the issue, Walter Maclaren was on the executive of the Manchester Society for Women's Suffrage alongside

R. M. Pankhurst, Emmeline's husband and another Congregationalist. Before women's suffrage became a prominent question in the public arena, Congregationalists were among its most energetic champions.

It is striking that, despite the frequency of Liberal governments during the period these men sat in the Commons, none of them achieved cabinet office. Henry Winterbotham, a barrister from Stroud in Gloucestershire who had displayed marked ability as a spokesman for Nonconformist claims during the passage of the 1870 Education Act, was in the following year appointed Under-Secretary of State for the Home Department.[26] It was widely expected that he would eventually reach the cabinet, but he died, still only thirty-six, in 1873. William Baxter, a Dundee merchant, was Secretary to the Admiralty and then Financial Secretary to the Treasury in Gladstone's first administration, but his chances of higher office were undermined by his inability to work with the Chancellor of the Exchequer, Robert Lowe. That was not unusual, for Lowe suffered from an unfortunate degree of intellectual contempt for other people, calling Baxter "a perfect cipher". Baxter's protest to Gladstone about Lowe's behaviour precipitated the removal of them both from office in 1873, and Baxter, though an MP down to 1885, did not serve again in government.[27] Caine was appointed a Civil Lord of the Admiralty in 1884 during Gladstone's second administration, but he was not reappointed in Gladstone's third term, and Caine's defection to the Liberal Unionists destroyed his further political prospects. Woodall was Surveyor-General of the Ordnance in the third administration and Financial Secretary to the War Office in the fourth, but would have been too old for office in the Liberal government of 1906 even if he had not died before. In 1907 Whitley was appointed a government whip and a year later Evans became Solicitor-General, but subsequently one took the Deputy Speakership before going on to be Speaker and the other assumed a senior legal appointment. Sir Joseph Compton-Rickett had hoped to secure a place in the government in 1906 through his role in the Free Church Council,[28] but had to wait a decade before he was selected by Lloyd George as Paymaster-General. The Congregational MPs were more likely to serve on royal commissions (ten did so) than to enter government, for they were often experts in particular fields, whether education, licensing or some professional speciality. Another role that three of them – Morley in 1871, Colman in 1872 and Mason in 1880 – fulfilled was to second the address of thanks to the crown at the opening of a session. This was regarded as an accolade for weighty back-benchers. When Mason, newly arrived in the Commons, delivered his speech in a strong Lancashire accent, it symbolised the true political significance of most of the Congregational MPs. They were generally not men suited for government, but representatives of the provinces.

It was in their home towns, not in parliament, that these individuals shone. Although some preferred to concentrate on business affairs, a large number served as councillors, often for extended periods. Edward Holden was a member of Walsall town council for more than sixty years. John Williams Benn was on the London County Council from its opening in 1889 and leader of the Progressives there from 1907 to 1918. At least twenty-three were chosen as alderman and at least thirty-six became mayor or provost. Several served more than one term as mayor, with George Leeman of York and Edward Gourley, a Sunderland shipowner, being chief magistrate three times and John Crossley, brother of Frank, and Joseph Leigh holding office as many as four times at Halifax and Stockport respectively. One of the MPs, the animal skin broker Thomas Challis, an alderman of the City of London since 1843, was its Lord Mayor ten tears later. It was a natural progression for men who held civic office to go on to represent the town in parliament. Not all the MPs did sit for their own constituencies. The officials of the Liberation Society, Miall and Williams, having no deep civic roots, were notable for seeking seats wherever they could find them. Others were placed in winnable constituencies at short notice. Thus Crosfield of Liverpool was drafted into Lincoln in 1886 when Ruston, the natural local leader and former MP, deserted Liberalism: his being a replacement Congregationalist probably dictated the choice. But most of those returned to parliament sat for the constituency in which they lived and did business. Thomas Rowley Hill, a Worcester manufacturer, was typical. He had been sheriff of the town in 1857 and mayor the following year. He unsuccessfully contested the constituency in 1868, but went on, remarkably, to win it in the year of Disraeli's triumph, 1874. He was again returned in 1880, but lost the seat in 1885 and did not recover it in a contest in the following year. At each general election there was a tightly fought struggle in Worcester against the Conservatives, with Hill the standard-bearer of the Liberal-Nonconformist section of the community. To be an MP was as much to hold a further civic office as it was to be a legislator.

Accordingly the Congregational MPs were usually deeply involved in the life of their towns and neighbourhoods. Local schooling was often a priority. Handel Cossham, a Bristol colliery proprietor, and James Pilkington, a Blackburn cotton manufacturer (to be distinguished from the glassmaker), set up British schools; Benjamin Armitage, a cotton spinner at Pendleton in Lancashire, established a half-time school there; Thomas Barnes, yet another cotton master, founded a school called "The Seminary" in Bolton. Several of the MPs found their way on to school boards after 1870, five of them becoming chairman, and Leigh and Ripley took a particular interest in promoting technical education. Secondary and higher education were also within their purview. Armitage was a trustee of Manchester Grammar School and Charles Reed sat on the committee of the City of London School. Richard was a spokesman for higher education in Wales, and W. H. Wills, the Bristol tobacco manufacturer, gave generously to his civic university. Especially in the earlier part of the century, the future MPs were sometimes patrons of the Mechanics' Institutes that offered evening classes to the workers. Thus Milligan, Ripley and Salt were all active in the Bradford Mechanics. Ripley was also first president of the Bradford Philosophical Society, an instance of the Literary and Philosophical Societies that catered for a higher social echelon and that other MPs supported as well. Several MPs gave generously to libraries, art galleries and museums. Colman, for example, gave a collection of books on the county to the Norwich library and bequeathed a number of landscapes of the Norfolk school to the art gallery. Frank Crossley presented a public park to Halifax and Barnes gave one to Bolton. Mason initially backed a scheme for a park in Ashton, but, with typical angularity, withdrew his support when a site was selected over the town boundary in Stalybridge. The Crossley Orphanage, founded by John as well as Frank, was a major Halifax institution, and other MPs contributed to equivalent organisations elsewhere. Their philanthropy often encompassed hospitals, and especially later in the period, children's wards. Almshouses, zoos, loan funds, female penitentiaries, convalescent homes and maternity homes all enjoyed the backing of at least one of the MPs. In all these ways, this group of men confirmed their credentials to be seen as local worthies. Their bounty made them more electable, but their motives were not so crass. As T. C. Taylor of Batley put it, "I was trained up both by my parents and at Silcoates School in the doctrine that 'None of us liveth to himself', and that our whole life should be a means of helping those less fortunate than ourselves."[29] They were deploying the resources they had been given for the common good.

Many of them were honoured for their public exertions. Twenty-one received knighthoods. The earliest was conferred on Charles Reed in 1874 for his distinguished chairmanship of the London School Board. Eight of the knighthoods were awarded during the 1906 parliament in which at last Nonconformity seemed to have come into its own. One of the MPs, Samuel Evans, received a GCB in 1917 after he had left parliament for his careful adjudications in maritime prize law during the war. Nine gained baronetcies, the first being awarded to Frank Crossley in 1863 as part of Palmerston's campaign to broaden the basis of honours to encompass industrialists. Crossley's eminence as an employer and philanthropist made him an obvious candidate for a public accolade. Only three, however, achieved a seat in the House of Lords. One was W. H. Wills, whose solid support for the Liberal cause in the West Country combined with his generous benefactions to Bristol marked him out as a prime candidate for ennoblement as soon as the Liberals entered office in 1906. He took his seat as Lord Winterstoke of Blagdon. The other peers were H. H. Cozens-Hardy, a career lawyer, who had served as Master of the Rolls for seven years when he became Lord Cozens-Hardy of Letheringsett, and John Jones-Jenkins, the Swansea Liberal Unionist, who was probably already an Anglican by the time he entered the Lords as Baron Glantawe in 1906. Perhaps, though, it was even more distinguished to have declined a peerage, as did Morley in 1885. Public recognition, then, did come the way of some of these men, often serving as an indication of the respect they had earned by their work for their communities.

The set of Congregational MPs might be charged with provinciality in the derogatory sense. J. S. Cheetham, a Stalybridge cotton master, used to amuse Lord John Russell by his anecdotes of Lancashire life delivered in the local accent.[30] Mason, with a similar penchant for Lancashire dialect literature, an uncritical self-confidence and an aggressively prominent unshaven chin, must have seemed an uncouth figure when he arrived in the Commons in 1880. These men, apart from some of the barristers among them, were not known for their contributions to parliamentary debate. Salt never spoke except on formal occasions like the presentation of a petition; Crosfield "had rather a gruff voice and was prone to be dull and prosy in his speaking"; Albert Spicer was no orator.[31] Here was a difference from the Methodists who entered parliament, most of whom, as local preachers, were practised public speakers. Among the Congregationalists, by contrast, though there were the four ex-ministers, only Compton-Rickett, Cossham and Goddard are known to have been lay preachers. Some of the Congregational MPs had a poor record of parliamentary attendance, no doubt primarily because of their provincial business responsibilities. The extreme case was Edward Crossley, nephew of Frank, who in the 1892 session did not vote in a single division.[32] Consequently the *Pall Mall Gazette* propagated an image of Nonconformist manufacturers who entered parliament lacking the intellectual and social qualifications for the position. James Guinness Rogers, Congregational minister and supreme commentator on late Victorian Liberalism, however, was at pains to dispel this notion. He pointed to Rowley Hill as "a true English gentleman, both in culture and style".[33] There were grounds for this alternative view. Wilks, a Fellow of the Royal Statistical and Zoological Societies, was a bibliophile whose collection was sold after his death at Sotheby's; Reed was a Fellow of the Society of Antiquaries who gathered manuscripts and keys; and Enoch Salisbury, a Chester barrister, assembled a comprehensive library on Wales. Some were pursuing the intellectual implications of their job, as when Edward Cook, a London soap boiler, became a Fellow of the Chemical Society, or Pellatt, the glassmaker, sat on the council of the School of Design. Others, however, were broader in their range of interests. Baines senior was the historian of Yorkshire, Lancashire, the Napoleonic Wars and the reign of George III. His son, Edward junior, was the chronicler of the cotton industry. Baxter, Caine, Frank Crossley and Leng published books on their observations of international travel. Brynmor Jones became an expert in the history of Wales. Edward Crossley erected an observatory and wrote a standard monograph on double stars. Sometimes, it is true, aspirations could outrun achievements. Compton-Rickett, who composed rather turgid novels, also supposed himself to be the successor to Herbert Spencer as England's leading philosophical thinker.[34] Nevertheless some of these figures received general acknowledgement of their expertise. Thus Evans, Jones, Leng and Reed were all awarded honorary doctorates for their intellectual attainments. Even if, as a group, the Congregational MPs were more notable for their communal service than for their cultural taste, they were not without their exponents of sweetness and light.

It is often hard to detect the theological views of the MPs, let alone to uncover their spirituality. Some of the earlier figures were inhibited in matters of faith. Edward Baines senior, who had originally worshipped in Leeds at the Unitarian Mill Hill Chapel, only joining the Congregational Salem Chapel in 1840, was asked eight years later on his deathbed whether he could entirely trust his soul to the Saviour. "*Yes*", Baines replied, "but I feel diffident in speaking of my own religious feelings, and wish not to use too strong expressions."[35] Milligan joined a church for the first time only while he was an MP,[36] and Salt, as we have seen, became a member only after his parliamentary service. Yet some of the group possessed a rich spiritual life. When Ruston prayed as deacon before a service in the vestry of Newland Congregational Church, Lincoln, his minister, J. D. Jones, found the experience uplifting. "Joseph Ruston", recorded Jones, "in the presence of God was like a little child."[37] There were men of strongly conservative theological convictions amongst the MPs. George Hadfield, the Manchester solicitor, was a stern opponent of Unitarians, indefatigably wresting control of Lady Hewley's Charity away from them. Edward Ball, the Conservative Cambridgeshire farmer, worked with the strongly Calvinistic C. H. Spurgeon, chaired a prayer meeting for revival and believed that education must be "based upon the Word of God".[38] J. S. Cheetham, as a deacon of Albion Chapel, Ashton, was "a man of strong Evangelical views, which he maintained with consistency, and yet with charity".[39] Morley, though not known for theological pronouncements, refused to support "what he believed to be false or inadequate representations of the Gospel of Christ".[40] On the other hand, there were men whose theological liberalism carried them beyond the bounds of Congregationalism: Wilson and Picton have been noted, but Keir Hardie also took this path. "Christianity today", he told the autumn assembly of the Congregational Union in 1892, "lay buried, bound up in the cerements of a dead and lifeless theology. It awaited decent burial, and they in the Labour movement had come to resuscitate the Christianity of Christ, to go back to the time when the poor should have the Gospel preached to them . . .".[41] The address, as Hardie had intended, caused a great stir. The majority of the MPs, however, seem to have followed the general theological trajectory of Congregationalism during this period. Cossham's views of the gospel, it was said in 1890, had "naturally become enlarged".[42] Likewise Compton-Rickett, though he left the City Temple when R. J. Campbell was expounding his radical "New Theology" there, was a broadening Evangelical.[43] Albert Spicer, according to his son, upheld the truths of Evangelical Christianity, "though he never liked the adjective".[44] The prevailing tone, at least from the closing years of the nineteenth century onwards, was one of liberal Evangelicalism.

The Congregational MPs usually shared the doctrinal opinions of their contemporaries because they were part and parcel of denominational life. Nine were sons of Congregational ministers, Brynmor Jones' father Thomas having occupied the chair of the Congregational Union in 1871-72. At least thirty were themselves deacons, with one, Caine, who was lay pastor, one, Langley, who was church secretary, and at least three who were church treasurer. Fifteen are known to have been Sunday school teachers, with one Christian Endeavour leader, and another four acted as Sunday school superintendents. Oldroyd returned to Dewsbury to conduct his men's Bible class each Sunday while he was serving at Westminster.[45] Some played a forceful part in church affairs. In the 1860s, for instance, Baxter successfully led the party demanding the introduction of organ music against stiff opposition at Ward Chapel, Dundee.[46] Again, many contributed large sums to their churches. In 1890 Abel Buckley, a cotton master of Ashton-under-Lyne, gave the tower and spire to the grand new Albion Chapel, promising to pay whatever proportion of the whole £40,000 cost of the site and building was not raised by the church.[47] Barnes, on retiring from Lancashire to the Quinta, near Oswestry in Shropshire in 1858, founded a Congregational Church, erected its building and maintained its minister at his own expense, thereby enabling the church to contribute freely to denominational funds and to support a missionary in Mongolia.[48] Certain churches were nests of MPs. Square Congregational Church, Halifax, nurtured three Crossley MPs and Park Church in the same town produced another three members, in this case unrelated to each other. Albion Chapel, Ashton, produced four MPs, but the prize for sending the largest contingent to Westminster goes to Horton Lane, Bradford, which moulded six. By and large, the MPs practised the polity they preached by participating fully in congregational life. Their active role in their local chapels was parallel to their work in their communities at large.

Inevitably the MPs were propelled into Christian organisations that operated on a wider stage. They chaired area or national Sunday School Unions, with Reed long being the animating force in the national body; they sat on the committees of the Religious Tract Society, the British and Foreign Bible Society and the Young Men's Christian Association, which Morley served from its inception; and, when Free Church Councils sprang up from the 1890s, MPs were to be found in their ranks, with Compton-Rickett playing a central role. In this period, however, they were even more active in denominational organisations. Several MPs were mainstays of county associations, with at least six acting as treasurer. Thirteen are known to have helped run the theological colleges, with Morley having contributed substantial donations to all eleven colleges in England and Wales. Morley was also treasurer of the Home Missionary Society, which in 1878 merged into the Congregational Church Aid Society. This body was the brainchild of Henry Lee, a Manchester manufacturer who was returned for Southampton in 1880, and who was a mainspring of most Union activities during the 1870s and 1880s. Lee, surprisingly, did not occupy the chair of the Congregational Union, but four others did: Henry Richard in 1877, Albert Spicer in 1893, Carvell Williams in 1899 and Compton-Rickett in 1907. Sixteen others sat on its council, and one on the Scottish equivalent. MPs were prominent as donors and trustees of the Memorial Hall that served as a denominational headquarters. Remington Mills, who opened the building in 1875, had given as much as £12,000 towards its erection.[49] A significant number of MPs also supported the London Missionary Society in its work overseas. Wilks had written *An Apology for the Missionary Society* as early as 1799 and Crosfield travelled to the Pacific on a tour of inspection of its stations. Likewise the Colonial Missionary Society sent Lee to Australia in the company of Alexander Hannay, the secretary of the Union. Spicer, who was chosen moderator of the International Congregational Council in 1899, remarked on his first election to parliament in 1892 that he represented two very enlightened constituencies, Monmouth Boroughs and the Congregational Union.[50] In truth, like Lee, Spicer was far more of a national figure as a Congregationalist than as an MP. Although the same could be said of few if any of the others, many of them took rank among the most committed Congregational laymen of their day.

The Congregational MPs of the nineteenth century, then, were men strongly rooted in their localities. They were civic figures who were preponderantly, in Robert Vaughan's terms, of the mercantile class. They were chiefly aspiring businessmen, but they were not merely individualists pursuing their own interests. Rather, they wished to carry their communities along with them as they prospered. Liberalism was the political choice of all but a handful because it seemed the party of progress for their fellow-townspeople as a whole. It was a vehicle for their own convictions about religious equality, but it was also a means of promoting education, peace, retrenchment and parliamentary reform, and increasingly of advancing social reform, that would benefit the Bradfords and Halifaxes of the land. The Congregationalists did not achieve high office at Westminster, but they did administer their home towns efficiently. They gave generously to the schools, parks and hospitals that would enhance municipal life and were often honoured for their achievements. They might be provincial in some of their ways, but in general they were by no means philistine. Their theology was mixed, reflecting their denomination, which they served both locally and, in many cases, nationally. Their Congregationalism, furthermore, did mould them. When Charles Bradlaugh, the militant secularist, was demanding to take his seat in the Commons during the early 1880s, Morley refused, on Christian grounds, to contemplate admitting an avowed atheist to the legislature. Morley felt so strongly that he offered to resign his Bristol seat if his Liberal constituents insisted on his endorsing Bradlaugh.[51] Lee, however, took a different line. He had refused to stand with Bradlaugh in Northampton, but felt that, according to Dissenting principles, a man's religious views should not disqualify him for public service. Accordingly Lee supported Bradlaugh's right to sit in parliament.[52] Morley and Lee voted in opposite lobbies, but they were both expressing convictions learned in Congregationalism. The MPs were embedded not just in their communities but also in their chapels.

NOTES

1   Winifred M. Bowman, *England in Ashton-under-Lyne* (Altrincham, 1960), p. 464.
2   Most of the evidence on which this analysis is based is derived from the catalogue of Congregational MPs in the nineteenth century published after the text of this lecture.
3   Viscountess Rhondda *et al.*, *D. A. Thomas, Viscount Rhondda* (London, 1921), pp. 32-3. J. Vyrnwy Morgan, *Life of Viscount Rhondda* (London, 1918), pp. 32-3.
4   Clyde Binfield, "Asquith: The Formation of a Prime Minister", *Journal of the United Reformed Church History Society* 2 (1981), p. 242.
5   Benjamin Nightingale, *Lancashire Nonconformity*, 6 vols (Manchester, 1890-93), Vol. 5, p. 322.
6   W. S. Fowler, *A Study in Radicalism and Dissent: The Life and Times of Henry Joseph Wilson, 1833-1914* (London, 1961), p. 24.
7   J. J. Leeman, Sir Joseph Leigh, W. S. B. McLaren, J. D. Peddie and T. F. C. E. Shaw.
8   Robert Balgarnie, *Sir Titus Salt, Baronet* (London, 1877), pp. 197-8, 140.
9   D. W. Bebbington, "Baptist M.P.s in the Nineteenth Century", *Baptist Quarterly* 29 (1981-82), pp. 3-24, at p. 3.
10 Robert Vaughan, *The Age of Great Cities* [1842] (London, 1969), p. 2.
11 J. D. Jones, *Three Score Years and Ten* (London, 1940), p. 43.
12 *Christian World*, 20 May 1909, p. 4.
13 Sidney Pollard and R. Turner, "Profit Sharing and Autocracy: The Case of J. T. and J. Taylor of Batley, Woollen Manufacturers, 1892-1966", *Business History* 18 (1976), pp. 4-34.
14 Albert Peel, *These Hundred Years: A History of the Congregational Union of England and Wales, 1831-1931* (London, 1931), p. 333.
15 *Dod's Parliamentary Companion* quoted in Michael Stenton and Stephen Lees (eds), *Who's Who of British Members of Parliament*, 4 vols (Hassocks, Sussex, 1976-81), Vol. 1, s.v.
16 Stenton and Lees (eds), *Who's Who*, Vol. 2, s.v.
17 F. H. Stead to W. E. Gladstone, 1 July 1892, Gladstone Papers, British Library, Add. MS 44515, f. 82.
18 I am grateful for this information to the Rev. Ivor Rees.
19 *Bradford Observer*, 11 November 1882, p. 7.
20 K. O. Morgan, *Wales in British Politics, 1868-1922*, 3rd edn (Cardiff, 1980), p. 25.
21 Bowman, *Ashton-under-Lyne*, p. 646n.
22 *Alliance News*, 7 September 1872, p. 648, quoted by Brian Harrison, *Drink and the Victorians* (London, 1971), p. 241.
23 C. J. James, *M. P. for Dewsbury* (Brighouse, Yorkshire, 1970), p. 114.
24 W. H. G. Armytage, *Heavens Below: Utopian Experiments in England, 1560-1960.* (London, 1961), p. 324.

25 Brian Harrison, *Dictionary of British Temperance Biography* (Coventry, 1973), p. 86.
26 J. P. Parry, *Democracy and Religion: Gladstone and the Liberal Party, 1867-1875* (Cambridge, 1986), pp. 296-7, 304-5.
27 James Winter, *Robert Lowe* (Toronto, 1976), pp. 289, 293.
28 Arthur Porritt, *More and More of Memories* (London, 1947), pp. 123-4.
29 Speech of 23 January 1937, quoted by Pollard and Turner, "Profit Sharing and Autocracy", p. 30n. 13.
30 John Stoughton, *Recollections of a Long Life* (London, 1894), p. 347.
31 Balgarnie, *Sir Titus Salt*, p. 189. Jones, *Three Score Years and Ten,* p. 51. [S. D. Spicer], *Albert Spicer, 1847-1934: A Man of his Time by One of his Family* (London, 1938), p. 38.
32 James, *M.P. for Dewsbury*, p. 112.
33 *Congregationalist*, September 1879, p. 706.
34 Harry Jeffs, *Press, Preachers and Politicians* (London, 1933), p. 145.
35 *Christian Witness*, 1851, p. 320.
36 *Bradford Observer*, 10 July 1862, p. 6.
37 Jones, *Three Score Years and Ten*, p. 43.
38 William Walters, *Life and Ministry of the Rev. C. H. Spurgeon* (Edinburgh, 1884), p. 101. *Wesleyan Times*, 20 February 1860, p. 117. *Dod's Parliamentary Companion*, 1857, quoted by Stenton and Lees (eds), *Who's Who*, s.v.
39 J. Guinness Rogers, *An Autobiography* (London, 1903), pp. 111-12.
40 J. C. Harrison, *Samuel Morley: Personal Reminiscences* (London, 1886), p. vii.
41 *Labour Prophet*, November 1892, quoted by K. O. Morgan, *Keir Hardie: Radical and Socialist* (London, 1975), p. 63.
42 C. A. M. Press, *Liberal Leaders of Somerset* (Bridgwater, 1890), p. 30.
43 *Christian World*, 30 December 1909, p. 2. Arthur Compton-Rickett, *Joseph Compton-Rickett: A Memoir* (Bournemouth, 1922), p. 136.
44 [Spicer], *Spicer*, p. 9.
45 *Christian World*, 1 July 1909, p. 2.
46 C. M. Falconer and J. C. Low, *A Hundred Years of Congregationalism: The Story of Ward Chapel*, privately printed (Dundee, 1934), pp. 55-6.
47 Nightingale, *Lancashire Nonconformity*, Vol. 5, pp. 304, 302.
48 Ernest Elliott, *Congregationalism in Shropshire* (Oswestry, 1898), pp. 280-8.
49 Peel, *These Hundred Years*, p. 277.
50 *Christian World*, 11 August 1892, p. 645.
51 W. L. Arnstein, *The Bradlaugh Case: Atheism, Sex and Politics among the late Victorians*, 2nd edn (Columbia, MO, 1984). p. 356.
52 *Congregationalist*, December 1880, p. 971.

Congregational MPs in the Nineteenth Century

A Catalogue

The catalogue that follows contains biographical data on the Congregationalists who sat in the House of Commons during the nineteenth century. The main list, which includes one hundred and two MPs, is the body of evidence on which the paper on *Congregational Members of Parliament in the Nineteenth Century* is based. There are indications, or at least reasonable grounds for the presumption, that each of them was a member of a Congregational church at some point during the period they served at Westminster. The one exception is Sir Titus Salt, who is known not to have become a church member until after he left the Commons but whose Congregational credentials are otherwise impeccable. There is also a supplementary list of supposed Congregational MPs who turn out to have been affiliated to another denomination or uncertain in their allegiance. Several might, on further investigation, turn out to be actual church members. No doubt one or two others have been missed, but the aim has been to present as comprehensive a listing as possible.

In each entry the dates of birth and death and period as an MP are given first. Then there are general biographical details culled, unless otherwise indicated, from the sources specified at the end of the entry. A further paragraph provides information about church membership and related activities. The reader might like to compare the equivalent listing of Baptist MPs published in *The Baptist Quarterly* 29 (1981-82), pp. 3-24, and discussed in a further article at pp. 51-64.

It is a pleasure to record thanks to the people named in the catalogue as having provided information. The extent of the debt to the editor of the *Journal of the URC Church History Society* will be evident from the number of times the initials 'JCGB' appear.

Abbreviations

BDEB   *The Blackwell Dictionary of Evangelical Biography, 1730-1860*, ed. D. M. Lewis, 2 vols (Oxford, 1995)

BDMBR   *Biographical Dictionary of Modern British Radicals*, ed. J. O. Baylen and N. J. Gossman, 3 vols (Brighton, 1979-88)

Boase   *Modern English Biography*, ed. Frederic Boase, 6 vols (Truro, 1892-1921)

BW   *The British Weekly* (London)
C   Conservative
CYB   *Congregational Year Book* (London)
CW   *The Christian World* (London)
DWB   *Dictionary of Welsh Biography down to 1940* (London, 1959)
Escott   Harry Escott, *A History of Scottish Congregationalism* (Glasgow, 1960)
FCYB   *Free Church Year Book* (London)
JCGB   Information from Professor J. C. G. Binfield
L   Liberal
LMS   London Missionary Society
LN   Benjamin Nightingale, *Lancashire Nonconformity*, 6 vols (Manchester, 1890-93)
LU   Liberal Unionist
Manning   B. L. Manning, *The Protestant Dissenting Deputies* (Cambridge, 1952)
ODNB   *Oxford Dictionary of National Biography*, ed. H. C. G. Matthew and Brian Harrison (Oxford, 2004)
Peel   Albert Peel, *These Hundred Years: A History of the Congregational Union of England and Wales, 1831-1931* (London, 1931)
Surman   Surman Index of Congregationalists, Dr Williams's Library, London
T   *The Times* (London)
WW   *Who's Who* (London)
WWBMP   *Who's Who of British Members of Parliament*, ed. Michael Stenton and Stephen Lees, 4 vols (Brighton, 1976-81)
WWW   *Who Was Who* (London)

List of Congregational MPs

WILLIAM ABRAHAM
    1840 - 2 Aug. 1915
    MP (N) for W Limerick, 1885-92
    Cork, NE, June 1893 - Jan. 1910
    Dublin Harbour, June 1910 - Aug. 1915

Born in Limerick. Chairman of Limerick Board of Guardians, 1882-83, 1885-86. Active in Irish Land League. Joint treasurer of Irish Nationalist Party. Moved resolution for removal of C. S. Parnell from the chairman-ship of the Irish Parliamentary Party, 6 Dec. 1890, precipitating split

(C. C. O'Brien, *Parnell and his Party, 1880-90* (Oxford, 1957), pp. 342-4). Of 26 Ashmount Road, Hornsey Lane, London.

Presumably member of Limerick Congregational Church. Possibly connected with Park Chapel, Crouch End, latterly (JCGB).

WWBMP 2. *WWW* 1897-1916.

BENJAMIN ARMITAGE
28 Feb. 1823 - 4 Dec. 1899
MP (L) for Salford, 1880-85
Salford, W, 1885-86

Cotton spinner of Manchester; partner in Sir Elkanah Armitage and Sons from 1844; eventually chairman. Son of Sir Elkanah Armitage, Congregationalist, mayor of Manchester 1848 and defeated candidate for Salford, 1857. Moravian School, Mirfield, and Barton Hall School, Patricroft, near Manchester. Helped Richard Cobden with details of commercial treaty with France, 1860. President of Manchester Chamber of Commerce, 1878-81. Prominent in Manchester Reform Club; president, 1876. Freeman of Salford, 1899. Contested Salford, W, in 1886 and 1892. Gave playground and half-time school to Pendleton. Trustee of Manchester Grammar School. Of Chomlea, Claremont Road, Pendleton.

Armitage and his family provided Congregational Sunday school at Pendleton. His sixth child married at Hope Chapel, Eccles, 1893. Therefore Armitage probably member there. (JCGB) Trustee of Lancashire Independent College from 1864, presiding at lunch to mark opening of extension, 1878 (Joseph Thompson, *Lancashire Independent College, 1843-1893: Jubilee Memorial Volume* (Manchester, 1893), pp. 180, 199). Trustee of Woodward Trust for ministers of small Lancashire Congregational churches (Benjamin Nightingale, *The Story of the Lancashire Congregational Union, 1806-1906* (Manchester, 1906), p. 102). Not in *LN*.

WWBMP. Boase. W. Haslam Mills, *The Manchester Reform Club, 1871-1921*, privately printed (Manchester, 1922), pp. 7 ff. *T*, 6 Dec. 1899, p. 7.

EDWARD BAINES (Sen.)
5 Feb. 1774 - 3 Aug. 1848
MP (L) for Leeds, Feb. 1834-1841

Born Walton-le-Dale, Lancs. Hawkshead and Preston Grammar Schools. Apprenticed to Preston printer, moved to Leeds, acquiring *Leeds Mercury,* 1801. In 1820s fought tithes, church rates and university tests and supported Catholic emancipation. Helped secure return of Henry

Brougham for Yorkshire, 1830, and T. B. Macaulay for Leeds, 1832. Replaced Macaulay in parliament in 1834. As MP supported ballot, suffrage extension, removal of religious disabilities and free trade, opposing regulation of factory hours (*contra ODNB*). Subsequently attacked state education. JP. Wrote histories of Yorkshire, Lancashire, Napoleonic wars and reign of George III. "The English Franklin". His oldest son Matthew Talbot Baines (1799-1860), who graduated from Trinity College, Cambridge, in 1820, and so was by then an Anglican, became MP (L) for Hull, 1847-52, and for Leeds, 1852-59, President of the Poor Law Board, 1849-55, and Chancellor of the Duchy of Lancaster in the cabinet, 1855-58 (*ODNB*). Of 2 Tanfield Court, Temple, London.

Worshipped in Leeds at Mill Hill Unitarian Chapel and Salem (East Parade) Congregational Chapel, which he joined 3 Jan.1840 through influence of wife, Charlotte. Attended Craven Chapel in London (JCGB). On his deathbed, marked by "patriarchal dignity" (*Christian Witness*, 1851, p. 321).

Sir Edward Baines, *The Life of Edward Baines* (London, 1851). Clyde Binfield, *So Down to Prayers* (London, 1977), pp. 65-72. *ODNB* (omitting religion). *BDEB. Christian Witness*, 1851, pp. 318-22.

Sir EDWARD BAINES
28 May 1800 - 2 Mar. 1890
MP (L) for Leeds, 1859-74

Proprietor of *Leeds Mercury*; partner with Edward Baines, sen., from 1827. New College, Manchester. Supported repeal of corn laws. Total abstainer from 1837. Opposed state education in 1840s. As MP proposed bills in favour of extending franchise, 1861, 1864, and 1865, and championed Nonconformist causes. Defeated at Leeds, 1874. Founder member of Leeds Literary and Philosophical Society. President of West Riding (later Yorkshire) Union of Mechanics' Institutes for 44 years. President of economic section of British Association, Leeds, 1858. Member of Taunton Commission on secondary education, 1864-67, switching to support national system of elementary education. Chaired Yorkshire College, 1880-87. JP, DL. Knight, 16 Dec. 1880. Author of *A Companion to the Lakes of Cumberland, Westmoreland and Lancashire* (1829); *History of the Cotton Manufacture in Great Britain* (1835); *The Life of Edward Baines* (1851); *Fifteen Years of Experience of Total Abstinence* (1852), attaining in revised edition of 1857 a circulation of 284,000. Of Headingley Lodge, Leeds.

At age of 28 became member of East Parade Congregational Chapel, Leeds, where subsequently served as Sunday school superintendent until became MP (*BDEB*).

Derek Fraser, "Edward Baines", in Patricia Hollis (ed.), *Pressure from Without in Early Victorian England* (London, 1974). Clyde Binfield, *So Down to Prayers* (London, 1977), pp. 72-100. J. R. Lowerson, "The Political Career of Sir Edward Baines, 1800-1890" (Leeds MA, 1965). *ODNB. BDEB.* Boase. Political correspondence at Duke University, N. Carolina. Papers at W. Yorkshire Archives Service, Leeds.

JABEZ SPENCER BALFOUR
4 Sept. 1843 - 23 Feb. 1916
MP (L) for Tamworth, 1880-85
Burnley, Feb. 1889 - Dec. 1892

Promoter of various firms, including Liberator Building Society, by the late 1870s the world's biggest. First mayor of Croydon, 1883-84. Member of Croydon School Board from 1874. JP. His firms collapsed in 1892, the crash of the Liberator destroying the savings of many Nonconformists. Balfour fled to Argentina, with which an extradition treaty was arranged in order to bring him back to England for trial in October 1895. Sentenced to fourteen years' imprisonment, he was released in 1906, becoming a journalist and then a mining engineer. Latterly of Burcot, Abingdon.

Spent youth at Church Street Baptist Church, NW London, where his mother, Mrs Clara Balfour, and his sister, Mrs Dawson Burns, remained members, but was himself a Congregationalist (*Freeman*, 1 July 1892, p. 457). Member of George Street Congregational Church, Croydon? Or possibly of West Croydon Congregational Church, where the minister, J. P. Wilson, suffered from "mental derangement" and died in 1893 (E. E. Cleal, *The Story of Congregationalism in Surrey* (London, 1908), p. 138), an episode possibly connected with the Liberator crash.

David McKie, *Jabez: The Rise and Fall of a Victorian Scoundrel* (London, 2004). *ODNB* (omitting Congregational allegiance). *WWBMP* 2.

EDWARD BALL
1793 - 9 Nov. 1865
MP (Protectionist C) for Cambridgeshire, 1852 - Jan. 1863

Farmer at Burwell, Cambridgeshire. Born at Hastings. Educated at Bromley, near Newmarket. DL. Favoured established church (*Nonconformist*, 28 July 1852, p. 583), but supported abolition of church rates, 1857. Opposed Maynooth Grant. "An earnest supporter of education based upon the Word of God" (1862). Attended Milton Club dinner, 16 Feb. 1852 (*Christian Reformer*, Mar. 1853, p. 193).

Member of Burwell Congregational Church, where the balls on the parapet are supposed to be a tribute to the family (JCGB). Worked with C. H. Spurgeon before the preacher moved to London (William Walters, *Life and Ministry of the Rev. C. H. Spurgeon* (Edinburgh, 1884), p. 101). Chaired special prayer meeting for revival in Exeter Hall (*Wesleyan Times*, 20 Feb. 1860, p. 117).

BDEB (though inaccurate about being Whig). *WWBMP.* Boase, citing *Gentleman's Magazine*, Dec. 1865, p. 802.

THOMAS BARNES
9 Dec. 1813 - 24 April 1897
MP (L) for Bolton,1852-57, Feb. 1861-68

Cotton manufacturer. 1874, firm became Thomas Barnes and Co. on a profit-sharing basis ("Pioneers of the Cotton Trade: The Barnes Family" *per* JCGB). By 1897, there were 4 mills, a warehouse and 2,000 employees. With his father and brother, founded day school, "The Seminary", in the town, 1837. JP, DL. Donor of Farnworth Park to the town, opened 1864. Chairman of Lancashire and Cheshire Railway. Supported ballot and triennial parliaments; "opposed to all grants of public money to religious bodies" (1867*).* On parliamentary committee of Liberation Society, 1854 (B. J. Mason, "The Growth of Combative Dissent, 1832-1859", Southampton MA, 1958, p. 144). Defeated at Bolton, 1857 and 1868. Contested Bury, 1859. Of Birch Hall, Farnworth, near Bolton, Lancashire. Moved to the Quinta, near Oswestry, Shropshire, 1858. JP and High Sheriff for Denbighshire. Leg amputated after carriage accident in 1851.

Member from age of 24, deacon and Sunday school superintendent of Farnworth Congregational Chapel; remained seatholder after transferring membership. Treasurer of Blackburn Independent Academy. Donor of building for Quinta Congregational Chapel, 1858, church being constituted in 1862; deacon 1863. Erected Sunday school and maintained ministry at own expense, freeing church to support missionary to Mongolia and give generously to denominational colleges, Pastors' Retiring Fund, Caterham School, London Congregational Union, Barnardo's Homes, etc. Treasurer of Salop Congregational Association, 1861-85, visiting weaker churches. (Ernest Elliot, *Congregationalism in Shropshire* (Oswestry, 1898), pp. 280-8).

WWBMP. Bolton Evening News, cutting from 1897 (*per* JCGB).

WILLAM EDWARD BAXTER
24 June 1825 - 10 Aug. 1890
MP (L) for Montrose District, Mar. 1855-85

Merchant; partner in Edward Baxter and Co. to 1870, and afterwards senior partner in W. E. Baxter and Co. Dundee High School, Edinburgh University. Succeeded Joseph Hume as MP for Montrose District. Secretary to Admiralty, Dec. 1868 - Mar. 1871. Financial Secretary to Treasury (outside cabinet), Mar. 1871 - Aug. 1873. PC, 24 Mar. 1873. DL. Author of *Impressions of Central and Southern Europe* (1850), *The Tagus and Tiber* (2 vols, 1852), *America and the Americans* (1855), *Hints to Thinkers* (1860) and many lectures. Of Kincaldrum, Dundee.

Member of Ward Chapel, Dundee, taking lead in introduction of organ and new hymn book, 1863-66 (C. M. Falconer and J. C. Low, *A Hundred Years of Congregationalism: The Story of Ward Chapel,* privately printed (Dundee, 1934), pp. 55-6). Not United Presbyterian, as suggested by I. G. C. Hutchison, *A Political History of Scotland, 1832-1924* (Edinburgh, 1986), p. 80.

ODNB. WWBMP. Boase.

Sir JOHN WILLLIAMS BENN
13 Nov. 1850 - 10 Apr. 1922
MP (L) for Tower Hamlets, St George's, 1892-95.
Devonport, Jun. 1904 - Jan. 1910

Proprietor of the *Cabinet Maker.* Member from 1889, vice-chairman from 1895 and chairman in 1904-05 of London CC; leader of Progressives, 1907-18. Specially concerned with development of tramways. Unsuccessful candidate for St George's, 1895; Deptford, 1897; Bermondsey, 1900; and Clapham, Dec. 1910. Knight, 1906. Bart, 1914. JP, DL. "[R]estraint and calculation were never strong points in his vivacious character" (Gardiner p. 190, quoted by *ODNB*). Of The Old Knoll, Blackheath.

Son of Julius Benn, Congregational minister. Named after John de Kewer Williams, minister of Old Gravel Pit, Hackney, 1874-94 (*CW,* 23 June 1904, p. 3). Scholar and teacher in Zion Chapel Sunday school, Hyde, Cheshire (F. J. Powicke, *A History of the Cheshire County Union of Congregational Churches* (Manchester, 1907), p. 206). Secretary of Sunday school, Ebenezer Congregational Church, St George's (*CW,* 23 May 1907, p. 3). Superintendent, Sunday school at Old Gravel Pit from 1889 (Surman). Member of Christ Church, Westminster Bridge Road, by 1896; non-resident member, 1901, perhaps then attending Upminster Congregational Church (*Christ Church... Its Services and Institutions, with Reports for 1896* and *1901 per* JCGB). Transferred membership, Mar. 1921, to Oxted Congregational Church, Surrey, which invited him, apparently unsuccessfully, to become deacon (Oxted church records *per* JCGB).

A. G. Gardiner, *John Benn and the Progressive Movement* (London, 1925). *ODNB* (omitting religion). *WWW* 1916-1928.

EDWARD HAMMOND BENTALL
    19 June 1814 - 7 Aug. 1898
    MP (L) for Maldon, Essex, 1868-74

Agricultural implement maker of Heybridge, Essex. Inventor of patent broadshare and subsoil plough. Sailor, designing new style of yacht hull. Built cars in early twentieth century. Captain commandant of 1st Essex Engineer Volunteers, 1861-71.

Probably not member of Maldon Congregational Church (JCGB). Perhaps member of Heybridge Basin, founded 1850?

John Leather, *The Salty Shore* (Lavenham, 1979), p. 151. Boase. *T*, 16 Aug. 1898, p. 8.

ADAM BLACK
    20 Feb. 1784 - 24 Jan. 1874
    MP (Whig) for Edinburgh, Feb. 1856-65

Bookseller in own name from 1807. Edinburgh High School; University of Edinburgh. Acquired *Encyclopaedia Britannica,* 1827, and founded Adam and Charles Black, publishers of *Who's Who* from 1848 and of Scott's novels from 1851. Twice assistant of Edinburgh Merchant Co., and master, 1831. Chairman of Edinburgh and Leith Shipping Co.; of Edinburgh and Leith Gas Co. from 1846; and of Edinburgh Cemetery Co., 1846-48. Member of town council, 1833-36 and again by 1840 until 1848, and city treasurer. Lord Provost of Edinburgh, 1843 and 1846. JP, DL. Resisted Church of Scotland campaign for church extension at public expense in 1830s, publishing *The Church its own Enemy* (1835). Supported T. B. Macaulay as MP, 1839-47; 1852-56. Favoured any measure which would "provide education for every child in the kingdom" (1865). Opposed campaign against Maynooth grant, so securing support of Whigs and Catholics. Opposed parliamentary reform, voting against Edward Baines' bills in parliament. Compromised on Edinburgh annuity tax for support of established clergy, 1860. Leading member of Voluntary Church Association and of Scottish Central Board of Dissenters, but favoured state aid for Ragged Schools. Member of Argyll Commission on Scottish education from 1864. Defeated at Edinburgh, 1865. Director of Edinburgh Zoological Gardens from 1839. First president of Philosophical Institution, 1845. Of 38 Drummond Street, Edinburgh, and Prior Bank, near Melrose.

Originally intended to enter Church of Scotland ministry, but parents became Congregationalists. Member of Argyle Square Congregational Church, Edinburgh (Nicolson, pp. 14, 37, 127-8, 229-30). Its building was erected by Black's father, an office-bearer. Church moved to become Augustine Church, George IV Bridge, 1861. Originally member of North College Street Independent Chapel, Edinburgh, 1803. On committee of Congregational Union of Scotland, 1814, 1817 and 1822 (W. D. McNaughton, *Early Congregational Independency in Lowland Scotland* (Glasgow, 2005), Vol. 1, pp. 499, 500). Member of Fetter Lane Independent Chapel, London, where he lived 1804-06. Regular attender of Westminster Chapel when in London in later years (JCGB).

Alexander Nicolson (ed.), *Memoirs of Adam Black* (Edinburgh, 1885). *ODNB. BDMBR* 2. *WWBMP.* J. C. Williams, "Edinburgh Politics, 1832-1852", Edinburgh PhD, 1972.

Sir JOHN BRIGG
21 Sept. 1834 - 30 Sept. 1911
MP (L) for Yorkshire, West Riding, N, Keighley, 1895-1911

Worsted spinner until 1890. Chairman of Bradford Advisory Board of United Counties Bank. Director of Leeds and Liverpool Canal. Provisional mayor of Keighley, 1882. Alderman of West Riding CC. JP, DL. Knight, 1909. Leg amputated and so addressed Commons sitting. Wrote on parliamentary questions for *CW*. Interested in Brontes. (*CW*, 5 Oct. 1911, p. 2). Published scientific pamphlets. FGS. Governor of Keighley Girls' Grammar School and Giggleswick School (W. T. Pike (ed.), *Contemporary Biographies* (Brighton, 1898), p. 105, *per* JCGB). His son John Jeremy (b. 1862), a barrister, was Congregational Sunday school superintendent and L candidate for Thirsk in 1906 (*CW*, 4 Jan. 1906, p. ii). Of Kildwick Hall, near Keighley.

Quaker family. Married Mary Anderton of Congregational family, 1860 (JCGB). Deacon of Devonshire Street Congregational Church, Keighley, where for 23 years Sunday school superintendent (*CW*, 11 Nov. 1909, p. 3). Contributed to building Devonshire Street chapel and manse, to Utley Congregational Chapel and to old chapel in Keighley High Street that became mission (David James, *Class and Politics in a Northern Industrial Town: Keighley, 1880-1914* (Keele, 1995), p. 56).

WWW, 1897-1916. *WWBMP* 2.

ABEL BUCKLEY
1835 - 23 Dec. 1908
MP (L) for Lancashire, SE, Prestwich, 1885-86

Cotton master. Chairman of Manchester and Liverpool District Banking Co. Mill Hill School; Owens College, Manchester. JP. Defeated at Ashton, 1874 and 1886. Of Ryecroft Hall, Ashton-under-Lyne.

Grandson of Nathaniel Buckley, founder of Congregationalism in Ashton-under-Lyne. His father, Abel Buckley sen. (d. 1865), was by 1859 senior deacon of Albion Chapel. Abel jun. on Albion's psalmody committee, 1866. (JCGB) Initiated movement for building new Albion Chapel, 1890 (Benjamin Nightingale, *The Story of the Lancashire Congregational Union, 1806-1906* (Manchester, 1906), p. 159), laying foundation stone as donor of tower and spire (*LN*, vol. 5, pp. 304, 302).

WWW 1897-1916. *WWBMP* 2.

NATHANIEL BUCKLEY
1821 - 23 Mar. 1892
MP (L) for Stalybridge, Mar. 1871-74

Cotton spinner of Ashton. Brother of Abel Buckley. Unmarried. JP, DL. Contested Stalybridge, 1868 and 1874. Of Alderdale Lodge, Droylsden.

In 1890, contributed £1,000 to Albion Chapel, Ashton-under-Lyne, where attended. Had joined Hugh Mason in purchase of Dukinfield Old Hall Chapel as Congregational place of worship, 1872. (*LN*, vol. 5, pp. 302, 313).

WWBMP. Boase.

Sir WILLIAM POLLARD BYLES
13 Feb. 1839 - 15 Oct. 1917
MP (L) for Yorkshire, West Riding, N, Shipley, 1892-95
Salford, N, 1906 - Oct. 1917

Proprietor of *Bradford Observer*. Member of Interparliamentary Union for Peace and Arbitration. Member of executive, Northern Counties Education League (*CW*, 4 Jan. 1906, p. iv). Vice-president of Land Nationalisation Society. Opponent of Boer War. Defeated at Shipley, 1895; and at Leeds, E, 1900. Knight, 1911. Of 8 Chalcot Gardens, Hampstead.

Member of Horton Lane Congregational Church, Bradford, by 1864. Active in Horton Lane Young Men's Mutual Improvement Society and proposed to Sarah Anne Unwin at its Book Society's summer picnic (JCGB). Son of William Byles, deacon of Horton Lane (Clyde Binfield, *So Down to Prayers* (London, 1977), p. 117). MP's brother was A. H. Byles, Congregational minister. Attended conference of Labour and Congregational MPs, 8 Feb. 1893 (Peel, p. 333). Claimed, however, that only conceit made man believe in immortality for himself. At 1906 election charged with being anti-religious, but defended by T. Rhondda Williams

(T. Rhondda Williams, *How I Found my Faith* (London, 1938), pp. 122-3). Although in list of candidates in *CW*, 4 Jan. 1906, p. iv, not in list of Free Church MPs at *CW*, 1 Feb. 1906, p. 5. In 1916 confessed that he expected "to die within the year with all his hopes shattered and with his old belief in immortality gone" (A. S. Rowntree to Mary Rowntree, 18 Jan. 1916, Ian Packer (ed.), *The Letters of Arnold Stephenson Rowntree to Mary Katherine Rowntree, 1910-1918,* Camden 5th series, Vol. 20 (Cambridge, 2002), p. 206). *WWW* 1897-1916. *WWBMP* 2. Cf. [F. G. Byles], *William Byles by his Youngest Son* (Weymouth, 1932).

WILLIAM SPROSTON CAINE
26 Mar. 1842 - 17 Mar. 1903
MP (L) for Scarborough, 1880-85
(LU) for Barrow-in-Furness, Apr. 1886-90
(L) for Bradford, E, 1892-95
(L) for Cornwall, NW, 1900 - Mar. 1903

Iron and tinplate merchant, 1861-78, and then held mining and iron interests, but in 1893 Shaw's Brow Iron Co. collapsed, losing him *c.* £40,000. Subsequently chairman of Central Cyclone Co., and, from 1901, of United Kingdom Temperance and General Provident Institution. Gibson's School, Wallasey, and Birkenhead Park School under the Rev. Richard Wall. JP. Contested Liverpool, Feb.1873 and 1874, and Tottenham, 1885. Civil Lord of the Admiralty, 1884. LU chief whip, 1886-90. Defeated as Independent L at Barrow on resigning as LU, July 1890. Defeated at Bradford, E, 1895. JP. Leading temperance reformer at Liverpool. Vice-president of United Kingdom Alliance. President of British Temperance League and (1884-1903) National Temperance Federation. Through Liverpool Permissive Bill Canvassing Association, induced Liberals to hold meetings away from public houses at 1868 election. Agitated against spirit ration in Royal Navy in 1880s (Brian Harrison, *Drink and the Victorians* (London, 1971), pp. 333, 345). As member of Royal Commission on Licensing Laws, 1896-99, supported Lord Peel's minority report, though it rejected local option, and so withdrew from candidacy at Kilmarnock (D. A. Hamer, *The Politics of Electoral Pressure* (Hassocks, Sussex, 1977), pp. 299, 301-2). Hon. secretary and treasurer of Anglo-Indian Temperance Association, 1888-1903. Member of Royal Commission on Indian Finance, 1895-96. Delegate to Indian National Congress, Calcutta, 1890, supporting extension of self-government. Favoured women's suffrage, free trade, disestablishment in Wales and Scotland, a small army and no treaties except commercial ones. On executive of

Liberation Society. Author of *Hugh Stowell Brown: A Memorial Volume* (1888); *A Trip round the World in 1887-8* (1888); *Picturesque India* (1890); *Local Option: A Handbook* (1885). Collected modern water colours. Of 42 Grosvenor Road, London.

Member of Myrtle Street Baptist Church, Liverpool, and then of Stockwell Baptist Church, London. Founder (1884) and lay pastor of Wheatsheaf Hall Mission, South Lambeth Road, London (Newton, pp. 13, 32, 129-30, 134), which was originally sponsored by Stockwell but affiliated to London Congregational Union, 1894, though "very few of our members had any more interest in Congregationalism than they had in Mormonism" (William Kent, *Testament of a Victorian Youth* (London, 1938), p. 103, quoted by Jeffrey Cox, *The English Churches in Secular Society: Lambeth, 1870-1930* (New York, 1982), p. 116). President of Congregational Total Abstinence Union (as well as Baptist equivalent). (*BDMBR* 3).

John Newton, *W. S. Caine, M. P.: A Biography* (London, 1907). *ODNB*. *BDMBR* 3. *WWW* 1897-1916. *WWBMP* 2. *T*, 18 Mar. 1903.

THOMAS CHALLIS
1 July 1794 - 20 Aug. 1874
MP (L) for Finsbury, 1852-57

Skin broker in Finsbury and hide and skin salesman in Leadenhall and Bermondsey markets. Steward of Butchers' Company of City of London, 1820; Master, 1839-40. Director of General Life and Fire Insurance Co. Unmarried. Alderman of City of London, 1843; sheriff of London and Middlesex, 1846-47; Lord Mayor, 1852-53. Encouraged schools of art. Favoured extension of franchise, equal electoral districts, short parliaments and ballot. Opposed all religious endowments including Maynooth (1857). Of 32 Wilson Street, Finsbury, and Enfield.

Baptised at Barbican Independent Chapel, where became deacon. Chairman of Sunday School Union. (http://www.london-city-history. org.uk/biography.htm)

WWBMP. Boase.

JOHN S CHEETHAM
1802 - 18 May 1886
MP (L) for Lancashire, S, 1852-59
Salford, Feb. 1865-68

Cotton manufacturer. Prominent in Anti-Corn Law League, "a shrewd, energetic man" with command of Lancashire dialect and knowledge of Lancashire life that gave amusement to Lord John Russell (John Stoughton,

Recollections of a Long Life (London, 1894), p. 347). Favoured suffrage extension, redistribution of seats and ballot; opposed all religious endowments (1867). Unsuccessful candidate at Huddersfield, 1847; Lancashire, S, 1859; Salford, 1868. JP. Established libraries and art galleries. Of Eastwood, Stalybridge, Cheshire.

Familiar with Moravians in youth (Stoughton, p. 347). Member of Albion Chapel, Ashton-under-Lyne, deacon and Sunday school teacher, taking class of young women; "a man of strong Evangelical views, which he maintained with consistency, and yet with charity" (J. Guinness Rogers, *An Autobiography* (London, 1903), pp. 109, 111-12). Later member of Stalybridge Congregational Church (JCGB). Donor to LMS fund for Indian extension, *c.* 1859 (Brian Stanley, " 'Commerce and Christianity': Providence Theory, the Missionary Movement and the Imperialism of Free Trade, 1842-1860", *Historical Journal* 26 (1983), p. 88 n.102).

WWBMP. Boase.

JEREMIAH JAMES COLMAN
14 June 1830 - 18 Sept. 1898
MP (L) for Norwich, Feb. 1871-95

Mustard manufacturer. Married Caroline, daughter of W. H. Cozens-Hardy, so that brother-in-law of H. H. Cozens-Hardy. Provided extensive welfare facilities for employees. Chairman of committee of independent reformers from 1859. Member of Norwich town council, 1859-71; alderman from 1896; sheriff, 1862-63; mayor, 1867-68. Sheriff of Suffolk from 1893. Promoted *Eastern Daily Press* from 1870. Seconded address to the throne, 6 Feb. 1872. JP, DL. Believed in putting historic buildings to public use. Trustee of Norwich Museum. Agriculturalist and breeder of stock. Of Carrow House, Norwich, and The Clyffe, Corton, near Lowestoft.

Member from 1856 and deacon from 1861 to 1870 of St Mary's Baptist Church, Norwich. Rented sittings at Bloomsbury Baptist Church, London, when young. On Baptist Missionary Society committee from 1864. Treasurer of Norfolk Association of Baptist churches until death. Under wife's influence had children baptised as infants in 1870 and transferred membership to Prince's Street Congregational Church in 1871. Nominated as deacon but declined to serve. Erected Free Methodist Chapel at Corton. First treasurer of Norwich YMCA; later president. Preferred "Christian work that is not hedged about by high denominational walls" (Colman, p. 143). Gave £3,000 to Prince's Street building fund, 1879-84 (church records *per* JCGB).

H. C. Colman, *Jeremiah James Colman: A Memoir*, privately printed

(London, 1905). *ODNB* (mentioning Baptist but not Congregational allegiance). *BDMBR* 3 ("lifelong Baptist"). *WWBMP* 2. Boase.

Sir JOSEPH COMPTON-RICKETT

13 Feb. 1847 - 30 July 1919
MP (L) for Scarborough, 1895-1906
Yorkshire, West Riding, E, Osgoldcross, 1906-18
Yorkshire, West Riding, Pontefract, 1918 - July 1919

Coal merchant, retiring 1907, and then flour miller (*CW*, 2 May 1907, p. 3). Chairman of Rickett, Cockerell and Co. Ltd and other companies. King Edward VI Grammar School, Bath. Approached by four constituencies to stand in 1895, whip recommending Scarborough. Favoured secular education. (*BW*, 16 Apr. 1896, p. 426). Delivered paper *in absentia* on the Christian idea of the state to the International Congregational Council at Boston, 1899 (*CW*, 28 Sept. 1899, p. 12). Started weekly column on "The Week in Parliament" in *CW*, 23 Jan. 1902, p. 1. Unsuccessfully sought government office in 1905 through Free Church Council (Arthur Porritt, *More and More of Memories* (London, 1947), pp. 123-4). Added "Compton" to surname, 1908. Knight, 1907. PC, 1911. DL. Paymaster-General, 1916-19. Author of *The Christ that is to Be* (1891); *The Quickening of Caliban* (1893); *The Free Churchman of Today* (1902); *Origins of Faith* (1909); *Congregationalism and Modern Life* (1916). Regarded himself as successor to Herbert Spencer as England's leading philosophical thinker (Harry Jeffs, *Press, Preachers and Politicians* (London, 1933), p. 145). Of Barham House, East Hoathly, Sussex (1907), and Wingfield, Bournemouth (1919).

Baptised in Church of England (*CW*, 3 Jan. 1907, p. 3). Married daughter of H. J. Gamble, Congregational minister (*CW*, 10 May 1906, p. 3). Of Croydon Congregational Church (Arthur Compton-Rickett, *I Look Back* (London, 1933), p.33). "He is associated with several forms of Nonconformity, especially as a benefactor, but is usually found worshipping with Congregationalists" (*CW*, 16 Jan. 1896, p. 49). Member and deacon of City Temple, leaving during New Theology controversy (*CW*, 30 Dec. 1909, p. 2). Had been close friend of Joseph Parker, at whose semi-jubilee in 1894 he presided (William Adamson, *The Life of the Rev. Joseph Parker, D.D.* (Glasgow, 1902), p. 246). Transferred to Brondesbury Park Congregational Church, NW London. Frequent lay preacher (Compton-Rickett, p. 134). Treasurer of Free Church Council and LMS. Chairman of Congregational Union, 1907. President of Free Church Council, 1915. Supporter of YMCAs, introducing a broader spirit (*BW*, 16 Apr. 1896, p. 426). A broadening Evangelical (Compton-Rickett, p. 136).

Arthur Compton-Rickett, *Joseph Compton-Rickett: A Memoir* (Bourne-mouth, 1922). *WWW* 1916-1928. *WWWBMP* 3.

EDWARD RIDER COOK
4 June 1836 - 21 Aug. 1898
MP (L) for West Ham, N, 1885-86

Soap boiler; senior partner in Edward Cook and Co., of East London Soap Works, Bow. Chairman of Animal Charcoal Co., 1883-93, and of London Riverside Fish Market Co., Shadwell, 1886-98. President of Society of Chemical Industry, 1890-91. Fellow of Chemical Society. City of London School; University College, London. Member of Metropolitan Board of Works, 1865-89. Defeated at West Ham, N, 1886. JP. Of Woodford House, Woodford Green, Essex.

Executor of Thomas Binney. Baptised at King's Weigh House, where at least two of his children baptised. Moved *c.* 1871 to Woodford Green, Essex, where joined Woodford Congregational Chapel. In 1875 led secession of Congregationalists and Baptists to join Free Methodists in forming Woodford Green Union Church, which affiliated to Essex Congregational Union in 1882. (JCGB).

WWBMP 2. Boase. *T,* 23 Aug. 1898, p. 3.

THOMAS COOTE
1850-
MP (L) for Huntingdonshire, S, 1885-86

Colliery factor at St Ives, Huntingdonshire. Unsuccessful candidate for Cambridgeshire, Mar. 1884, and Huntingdonshire, S, 1886. Of Ambury House, Huntingdon.

Coote's father, another Thomas, was treasurer of the Huntingdonshire Union of Independent and Baptist Churches, and in 1886 Thomas junior succeeded him in that office (*CYB,* 1862, p. 123, and 1886, p. 300). The father was a leader of a Congregational separation from the Fenstanton Union Church in the 1870s and on the Congregational Union committee by 1870 (*CYB,* 1870, p. ix). At Huntingdon, where Thomas jun. lived, he would have been a member of Trinity Union Church. (JCGB) The Baptist preponderance in that church would explain why the *Freeman,* 18 Dec. 1885, p. 838, supposed him to be a Baptist.
WWBMP 2.

HANDEL COSSHAM
31 Mar. 1824 - 23 Apr. 1890
MP (L) for Bristol, E, 1885-90

Bristol colliery proprietor. Employed *c.* 1,500 at Parkfield and Kingswood collieries. Named after the composer, his father's favourite. Spoke at Anti-Corn Law meeting in Stroud addressed by Cobden and Bright, 1842. Supported North in American Civil War, visiting the United States at its conclusion. Member of Bath town council; mayor, 1882-83 and 1884-85. Member of Bristol town council, 1864-70. Contested Nottingham, May 1866; Dewsbury, 1868; Chippenham, 1874. Built British School in Thornbury, 1862, and donated Cossham Hall, 1888. Organised classes in mining engineering, his campaign for instruction in science and technology in Bristol leading to foundation of university (Meller, pp. 177, 58). Published geological and political pamphlets. Fellow of the Geological Society, 1855. Cossham Hospital, Kingswood, Bristol, founded under his will, opening 1907. Died at National Liberal Club after being taken ill in Commons. Of Weston Park, Bath, and Holly Lodge, Bristol.

Active at Mangotsfield Tabernacle, *c.* 1851 (*CYB*, 1891, p. 11). Baptised at Stroud Congregational Church. In 1842 joined Thornbury Congregational Church, where had been Sunday school speaker for two years. Temperance activist from 1837. Lay preacher from 1844: "while his views as to the Gospel have naturally become enlarged, he has never ceased to regard that Gospel as the great lever by which the human race is to be raised" (Press, p. 30). Conducted Bible class in home on Sunday afternoons. Speaker at Congregational Commemoration of Great Ejection, 1862 (Peel, p. 240).

C. A. M. Press, *Liberal Leaders of Somerset* (Bridgwater, 1890), pp. 24-37. *WWBMP* 2. Boase. Helen Meller, *Leisure and the Changing City* (London, 1976). C. J. James, *M.P. for Dewsbury* (Brighouse, Yorks, 1970), pp. 65-81. Papers at Bristol Record Office.

HERBERT HARDY COZENS-HARDY
22 Nov. 1838 - 18 June 1920
MP (L) for Norfolk, N, 1885-99

Barrister. Amersham Hall School and University College, London. Called to bar, Lincoln's Inn, 1862. QC, 1882. Judge and knight, 1899. Lord Justice of Appeal and PC, 1901. Master of the Rolls, 1907-18. Baron Cozens-Hardy of Letheringsett, June 1914. JP. Elected chairman of general council of bar. Chairman of Council of Legal Education. Member of senate of London University and fellow of University College, London. Prepared to extend Sunday closing to England and favoured changing constitution of Lords (1899). Of Letheringsett Hall, Norfolk.

Brought up Wesleyan, his father becoming Wesleyan Reformer and helping to bring union with Wesleyan Methodist Association to create United

Methodist Free Churches (*CW*, 2 May 1895, p. 330). Attended Bloomsbury Baptist Church, 1854, and communicant 1856. Married at Grafton Square Congregational Church, Clapham, 1866. Attended Kensington Chapel from 1866 (MS autobiography), occasional communicant from 1868 and by 1898 considered to have been a member since 1868. (JCGB) Elected deacon in 1876 but declined to serve (John Stoughton, *Congregationalism in the Court Suburb* (London, 1883), p. 108). At Holt in Norfolk attended UMFC. President of Holt and District Free Church Council (*Free Church Record,* 1899, p. 53). Transferred membership to Whitefield's Tabernacle, 1907 (JCGB), where frequently spoke (*ODNB*). Brother-in-law of J. J. Colman (H. C. Colman, *Jeremiah James Colman: A Memoir,* privately printed (London, 1905), pp. 108-9, 306-7). Father-in-law of Charles Silvester Horne (W. B. Selbie, *The Life of the Rev. Charles Silvester Horne, M. A., M. P.* (London, 1920), p. 75).

ODNB (wrongly supposing father was Congregationalist). *WWBMP* 2. MS autobiography in Norfolk Record Office.

JOSEPH CRAVEN

1825-1914

MP (L) for Yorkshire, West Riding, N, Shipley, 1885-92

Worsted manufacturer, retiring 1875. Member of Thornton School Board and council of Bradford Chamber of Commerce. Governor of Thornton Grammar School and Crossley Orphanage. Of Ashfield, Thornton, near Bradford.

Member of Horton Lane Chapel, Bradford (A. W. Roberts, "The Liberal Party in West Yorkshire, 1885-1895 (with an epilogue, 1895-1914)", Leeds PhD, 1979).

WWBMP 2.

WILLIAM CROSFIELD

1838 - 17 May 1909

MP (L) for Lincoln, 1892-95

Sugar boiler and refiner. Deputy Chairman of Liverpool Mortgage Insurance Co. Royal Institution School, Liverpool. Member of city council, Mersey Dock Board, Liverpool Education Committee. JP. Unsuccessful candidate for Warrington, 1885; Lincoln, 1886 and 1895. Temperance reformer. Member of Liberation Society. In consultations of Congregational and Labour MPs, 1892-93 (Peel, p. 333). Treasurer of the British, Continental and General Federation for the Abolition of Government Regulation of Prostitution, 1875. Governor of University College,

Liverpool, and co-founder of Gladstone Chair of Classical Literature and History, 1881 (Liverpool University e-calendar). Was difficult to persuade electors in 1892 that he was a teetotaller: "Water", they said, "never gave him that nose." (J. D. Jones, *Three Score Years and Ten* (London, 1940), p. 51). "Though of a choleric temperament he was a genial and sympathetic character" (*CW*, 20 May 1909, p. 4). Of Annesley, Aigburth, Liverpool. Member of Great George Street Congregational Church, Liverpool. Member of committee of Congregational Union by 1870 (*CYB*, 1870, p. ix); treasurer, 1894-1909, and on many committees. Friend of Pleasant Sunday Afternoon movement. Worked for Ragged Schools. Director of LMS, once undertaking deputation tour of Pacific. On building committee of Mansfield College, Oxford (*Mansfield College, Oxford: Its Origin and Opening* (London, 1890), p. 240). Brother-in-law of Samuel Pearson, Congregational minister (JCGB).

WWBMP 2. B. G. Orchard, *Liverpool's Legion of Honour* (Birkenhead, 1893), p. 258.

EDWARD CROSSLEY

1841 - 21 Jan. 1905

MP (L) for Yorkshire, West Riding, N, Sowerby, 1885-92

Carpet manufacturer, inheriting firm from his father Joseph Crossley at 27. Director and chairman of John Crossley and Sons Ltd. Owens College, Manchester. Alderman of Halifax; mayor 1874-76, 1884-85. On Liberation Society executive, 1886. Completed Arden Road almshouses, Halifax, started by his father. Fellow of the Royal Astronomical Society, 1867. Erected observatory and co-author of *Handbook of Double Stars* (1879). Because of air pollution, donated his telescope to Lick Observatory, California, 1895. (Wikipedia)

Member of Square Chapel, Halifax, and deacon, 1872-89. Previously attended Park Congregational Church, Halifax, from its opening in 1869. His wife taught in Square Chapel Sunday school. In 1889 resigned over minister's views on atonement, then helping to found Heath Congregational Church, Halifax. In 1893, retired to Isle of Wight, setting up independent Evangelical church at Ryde. (JCGB) Nephew of John Crossley, son-in-law of Edward Baines, jun., and brother-in-law of Wrigley Willans (J. C. G. Binfield, *So Down to Prayers* (London, 1977), p. 160).

WWBMP 2. Dale Johnson, "Eric Lawrence, Edward Crossley and the Conflict at Square Church, Halifax", TS (1990). Eric Webster, *Dean Clough and the Crossley Inheritance* (Halifax, 1988). John Hargreaves, "Religion and Society in the Parish of Halifax, c. 1740-1914" (Huddersfield Polytechnic PhD, 1991).

Sir FRANCIS CROSSLEY
26 Oct. 1817 - 5 Jan. 1872
MP (L) for Halifax, 1852-59
West Riding, 1859-65
West Riding, N, 1865-72

Carpet manufacturer, owning largest carpet factory in the world at Dean Clough Mills, Halifax. Drew large income from licences under patents. Firm became limited company 1864, when shares were issued to many employees. Built almshouses at Halifax, 1855. Presented park to town, 1857. Built orphanage and school on Skircoat Moor, 1860. Founded loan fund for deserving tradesmen of Halifax, 1870. Vice-president of Working Men's Club and Institute movement. JP, DL. Bart, 1863. Supported ballot (1871). Author of *Canada and the United States*, 1856. Bought Somerleyton Hall, Suffolk,1863. Of Belle Vue House, Halifax, and Somerleyton.

Member of Square Chapel, Halifax (probably). Laid its foundation stone and paid for its spire. Maintained Somerleyton Union Church, Suffolk. (JCGB) Supporter of LMS, to which he gave £20,000 in 1870, Congregationalist Pastors' Retiring Fund and a fund for widows of Congregational ministers, to each of which he gave £10,000.

ODNB. WWBMP. Boase. John Hargreaves, "Religion and Society in the Parish of Halifax, *c.* 1740-1914" (Huddersfield Polytechnic PhD, 1991).

JOHN CROSSLEY
16 May 1812 - 16 Apr. 1879
MP (L) for Halifax, 1874 - Feb. 1877

Carpet manufacturer; senior partner, 1837; chairman, 1864-77. Governing director of John Worsley and Son's Co., and chairman of Halifax Commercial Banking Co. Favoured religious equality. Mayor of Halifax, 1849, 1850, 1861 and 1862. JP. Joined brothers Sir Francis and Joseph in building orphanage, 1860. Of Broomfield, Halifax; and then Manor Heath, Halifax (1876).

Member of Square Chapel, Halifax, from 1833; deacon from 1836 (Hargreaves, p. 174). Associated with Square Sunday school from 1829. Chairman of Congregational Chapel Building Society. Trustee of Memorial Hall. Treasurer of Halifax District of Yorkshire Congregational Union. Chairman of committee, Silcoates School, 1875-79. Donor to Rotherham College. (JCGB) Presided at table at opening of Homerton College, 1852 (*Illustrated London News,* 1 May 1852).

WWBMP. Boase. John Hargreaves, "Religion and Society in the Parish of Halifax, *c.* 1740-1914" (Huddersfield Polytechnic PhD, 1991).

ALFRED DAVIES
1848 - 27 Sept. 1907
MP (L) for Carmarthen District, 1900-06
Founder of international carriers and underwriters, Davies, Turner and Co. Ltd, of London, Liverpool and elsewhere, with sister firm in United States. Member of first London CC, 1889-92. JP. Of The Lothians, Fitzjohns Avenue, Hampstead.

Son of John Davies, Congregational minister. Mill Hill School (after The Cedars, Rickmansworth). One of first deacons of Lyndhurst Road Congregational Church, Hampstead. (*CW*, 3 Oct. 1907, p. 3). Resigned as deacon due to "other xtian work . . . to which I am specially called, and in which I believe I can be more useful" (Church records, Lyndhurst Road, 2 Dec. 1886, *per* JCGB). That Christmas he and his wife gave their minister R. F. Horton a two-volume edition of Stanley's *Life of Thomas Arnold* (JCGB). In the habit of asking ministers to speak audibly (*CW*, 16 July 1903, p. 3).
WWW, 1897-1916. *WWBMP* 2.

Sir WILLIAM DAVIES
Aug. 1821 - 23 Nov. 1895
MP (L) for Pembrokeshire, 1880-92
Solicitor in Haverfordwest; senior partner in W. and W. Rees Davies and Co., Old Jewry, London, 1875-90. Founder of *Haverfordwest and Milford Haven Telegraph,* 1854. Had interests in Transatlantic Steam Co. Ltd. On Haverfordwest borough council for thirty years; alderman, 1858-83; mayor for two years. Conservative agent, Haverfordwest, Fishguard and Narberth Boroughs, 1851. (Information from the Rev. I. T. Rees) Contested Pembrokeshire, June 1876. Spent more than £20,000 for Liberal Party in Pembrokeshire. Vice-president, Pembroke and Haverfordwest Infirmary. JP, DL. Knight, 1893. Of Scoveston, Pembrokeshire.

Congregationalist (K. O. Morgan, *Wales in British Politics, 1868-1922*, 3rd edn (Cardiff, 1980), p. 40n.). But his first wife, who died in 1872, was buried in Macpelah Baptist Cemetery; he was trustee of Haverfordwest Baptist College; and he gave to Baptist churches at Broadhaven and Thornton. In 1874 he inherited estate of his partner, William Rees, a patron of Baptists. (M. J. Williams, former secretary of the Baptist Union of Wales). Nevertheless he seems to have been an Independent.
WWBMP. Boase. *T*, 25 Nov. 1895, p. 9.

FREDERICK DOULTON
1 June 1822 - 21 May 1872
MP (L) for Lambeth, May 1862-68

Manufacturer of earthenware goods. Member of Metropolitan Board of Works, 1856-72. Contested Reigate, Feb. 1858. Supported franchise extension, ballot, repeal of church rates and "the economical application of the public revenues" (1867). Of High Street, Lambeth, and Alleyn House, Dulwich Common, Surrey.

Baptised at Locks Fields Independent Chapel, York Street, Walworth (www.ryeland.com/tim/tree/f40.htm#f100). Attended Westminster Chapel (JCGB).

WWBMP. Boase.

Sir JAMES HASTINGS DUNCAN
Mar. 1855 - 31 July 1928
MP (L) for Yorkshire, West Riding, E, Otley, 1900-18

Worsted spinner; director of Ackroyd's Ltd. Chairman, Otley School Board. Alderman, West Riding CC. Knight, 1914. Of Kineholm, Otley, Yorkshire.

Deacon of Otley Congregational Church for over twenty-five years; Sunday school teacher and treasurer; trustee. Delegate to Congregational Union. (*CW*, 2 July 1914, p. 2).

WWW, 1916-1928. *WWBMP*, 2.

WILLIAM ECCLES
1794 - 17 June 1853
MP (L) for Blackburn, 1852 - Feb. 1853 (unseated on petition)

Cotton spinner. Practised as attorney for twenty years down to 1840. Active in Reform agitation in Blackburn and chairman of committee to return William Feilden in 1832. Chairman of Blackburn Anti-Corn Law Association, 1841-46. Favoured extension of suffrage, ballot, system of national education (1853). Of 8 Salisbury Street, London; and Spring Mount, Blackburn.

Member from 1817 of Chapel Street Independent Chapel, Blackburn; deacon, 1821-27. Buried in its yard with a monument. (W. A. Abram, *A Century of Independency in Blackburn* (Blackburn, 1878), pp. 43-6).

WWBMP.

Sir SAMUEL THOMAS EVANS
4 May 1859 - 13 Sept. 1918
MP (L) for Glamorgan, Mid, Feb. 1890-1910

Barrister. Collegiate School, Swansea; Aberystwyth University College; London University, LLB. Solicitor, Neath, 1883, entering town council.

Called to bar, Middle Temple, 1891; bencher, 1908. QC, 1901. Recorder of Swansea, 1906-08. Solicitor-General, 1908-10. President of Probate, Divorce and Admiralty Division of High Court, 1910, conducting prize court with distinction during First World War. Argued against women's suffrage. According to Stuart Rendel, "a lawyer on the make" (K. O. Morgan, *Wales in British Politics, 1868-1922*, 3rd edn (Cardiff, 1980), p. 113). JP. Knight, 1908. PC, 1910. GCB, 1917. Freeman of Swansea and Neath. Hon. LLD, Wales. Of Neath, Glamorgan.

Deacon of Skewen Welsh Independent Church, near Neath. Nephew of Evan Evans, Independent minister. Spoke for Union of Welsh Independents. (*CW* , 6 Feb. 1908, p. 3). Parents wished him to enter ministry, but preferred law (Information from the Rev. I. T. Rees). Member of Congregational Union committee (*CYB*, 1898, p. xiii). Married at King's Weigh House (*CW*, 9 Feb. 1905, p. 3). Frequently attended Welsh Tabernacle, King's Cross, under H. Elvet Lewis (*CW*, 23 Jan. 1908, p. 3).

ODNB (not mentioning religion). *DWB*.

WWBMP 2. MSS at National Library of Wales.

JOHN FENTON
c. 1791 - 25 July 1863

MP (L) for Rochdale, 1832-35, Apr. 1837 - July 1841

Banker at Rochdale. Supported New Poor Law, 1834, leading to loss of seat in 1835. His son William, also a Congregationalist, was candidate for NE Lancashire in 1868. Of Crimble Hall, near Bury, Lancs.

Member of Bamford Independent Chapel. Laid foundation stone of Heywod Independent Chapel, Good Friday 1835. (*LN*, vol. 3, pp. 261, 264).

WWBMP. Boase.

Sir DANIEL FORD GODDARD
17 Jan. 1850 - 6 May 1922

MP (L) for Ipswich, 1895-1918

Secretary of Ipswich Gas Company, 1877-87, and chairman from 1887. Educated at Stoke Hall, Ipswich, and Hastings. Civil engineer from 1867. Member of Ipswich town council, 1886-95; alderman from 1895; mayor, 1891-92. Candidate at Ipswich, 1892. Supported electoral, poor law and licensing reforms (1918). JP. Knight, 1907. PC, 1916. Had a "slightly brusque manner" (*CW*, 14 Nov. 1907, p. 3). Of Oak Hill, Ipswich.

Deacon by 1894 of Tacket Street Congregational Church, Ipswich; Sunday school teacher, Bible class leader and lay preacher (JCGB). Secretary, Suffolk Congregational Union. Member of committee, Congregational

Union, 1889-1900 (*CYB*). Treasurer of Congregational Church Aid Association (Surman). Regularly presided over Sunday evening men's own meetings at Ipswich Social Settlement, which he founded in 1896 and on whose buildings he spent £11,000 (*BW,* 14 Nov.1907, p. 141). Founded "For God and the People" movement (JCGB).

WWW 1916-1928. *WWBMP.*

Sir EDWARD TEMPERLEY GOURLEY
8 June 1828 - 15 Apr. 1902
MP (L) for Sunderland, 1868-1900

Shipowner. Alderman of Sunderland; three times mayor, last time in 1868. JP, DL. Knight, 1895. For 10 years captain, N. Durham Rifle Volunteers, and for 20 years commandant, Sunderland Rifles. Promoted Anglo-French naval relations, 1866. Of Cleadon, near Sunderland.

Brought up in Sans Street Baptist Church, Sunderland (*Baptist Magazine,* May 1874, p. 277). Member of Grange Congregational Church, Sunderland (Geoffrey Milburn, *Church and Chapel in Sunderland, 1780-1914* (Sunderland, 1988), p. 18).

WWW 1897-1916. *WWBMP. Baptist Magazine,* May 1874, p. 277.

GEORGE HADFIELD
28 Dec. 1787 - 21 Apr. 1879
MP (L) for Sheffield, 1852-74

Attorney, practising in Manchester. Son of Sheffield manufacturer. Author of *The Manchester Socinian Controversy* (1825) and chief mover against Unitarians in Lady Hewley suit. Opposed church rates at Manchester, 1833-35. Unsuccessful candidate for Bradford, 1835. A founder of Anti-Corn Law League. Introduced Qualifications for Offices Abolition Act (1866), eliminating some religious tests. Supporter of peace movement, financial and parliamentary reform; opposed to all religious endowments and union of church and state (1873). Prime mover in Rusholme Road Proprietary Cemetery, the first cemetery company to be set up in England. According to a former pastor, a "stern, unbending integrity gave to his decisions and proceedings an appearance of self-will and ruggedness of temper" (Griffin, p. 271). Of Victoria Park, Manchester.

Member successively of Grosvenor Street, Rusholme Road, Salford and Rusholme Road Independent Chapels (JCGB). Although he was founder of Rusholme Road, he withdrew from church in dispute over Sunday school (Griffin, pp. 264-6). Once connected with Patricroft Congregational Chapel. Laid foundation stone of Rusholme Congregational Chapel.

(*LN,* Vol. 5, pp. 14, 164) Secretary of Lancashire Congregational Union, 1811-17 (W. G. Robinson, *A History of the Lancashire Congregational Union, 1806-1956* (Manchester, 1955), p. 174). Gave £10,000 for the erection of 100 Independent chapels from 1864. Co-founder of Lancashire Independent College, giving £2,000 towards building at Whalley Range, Manchester, 1840.

ODNB. BDEB. BDMBR 2. *WWBMP.* James Griffin, *Memories of the Past* (London, 1883), pp. 271-82. *T,* 23 Apr. 1879. MS autobiography in Manchester Public Library. Letters in Joshua Wilson Papers, Congregational Library.

JAMES KEIR HARDIE
15 Aug. 1856 - 26 Sept. 1915
MP (ILP) for West Ham, S, 1892-95
Merthyr Tydfil, 1900 - Sept. 1915

Labour leader. Without formal education, down mine from 1866. County agent for Lanarkshire Miners' Union, 1879; then for Ayrshire. Editor, *Cumnock News,* 1882-86. Secretary of Scottish Miners' Federation, 1886. By end of 1887 had moved from Liberalism to ethical socialism. Chairman of Scottish Labour Party, 1888. Independent Labour candidate for Mid-Lanarkshire, 1888; for West Ham, S, 1895; for Bradford, E, Nov. 1896; and for Preston, 1900. Founder of *Labour Leader,* 1889. Chairman of Independent Labour Party, 1893-1900 and 1913-15; of Labour Representation Committee, 1900; and of Labour Party in Commons, 1906-07. Visited India and Australia, 1907. Supported women's suffrage. Author of *From Serfdom to Socialism* (1907) and various addresses. Collected ballad and chapbook literature of Scotland. Of 10 Nevill's Court, London EC; and Lochnorris, Cumnock, Ayrshire. The architect of the Labour Party.

Converted to Christianity, 1878 (Benn, p. 18). Joined Hamilton EU Church, transferring to Cumnock Congregational Church, 9 July 1882. (Church records *per* Dr W. D. McNaughton) Supported its minister, Andrew Scott, in dispute with deacons and so resigned membership, 23 Mar. 1884. Hired a hall, invited visiting preachers (Benn, pp. 33-4) and took lead in founding, 31 Aug. 1884, Cumnock EU Church, which lasted until 1895 (Escott, p. 328). As new MP, addressed autumn assembly of Congregational Union provocatively at Bradford, October 1892. Author of *Labour and Christianity: An Address* (London, 1910).

K. O. Morgan, *Keir Hardie: Radical and Socialist* (London, 1975). Caroline Benn, *Keir Hardie* (London, 1997). *ODNB* (mistakenly claiming Hardie left Evangelical Union Church in 1884). *WWW,* 1897-1916.

WALTER HAZELL
1843 - 12 Feb. 1919
MP (L) for Leicester, Aug. 1894-1900

Printer and publisher; head of Hazell, Watson and Viney of London and Aylesbury. Member of Holborn council, and mayor, 1911-12. Defeated at Leicester, 1900. JP. Commissioner of income tax. Chairman and treasurer of Peace Society. Treasurer of British Institute of Social Service. Treasurer of Land Law Reform Association. Joint founder of Self-Help Emigration Society and Children's Fresh Air Mission. Chairman, Women's Settlement, Canning Town. Chairman, Emigration Committee of Central Unemployed Body. President, Bloomsbury House Club and of Cartwright Gardens Ladies' Club. Chairman, Homes for Little Boys at Farningham and Swanley. Established training farm for the unemployed at Longley, Essex, 1896 (W. H. G. Armytage, *Heavens Below* (London, 1961), p. 324). Supported Liberator Relief Fund and Bridge of Hope Mission (*CW*, 21 Mar. 1912, p. 3). Of 9 Russell Square, London, and Walton Grange, Aylesbury.

His mother, Martha, was a daughter of John Lane, Presbyterian then Congregational minister. His father, Jonathan Hazell, was deacon of Park Chapel, Crouch End, from 1858, and so was his father-in-law, James Tomlin. Walter became Sunday school teacher there and deacon from 1868. ([W. H. Groser], *Park Chapel, Crouch End: Jubilee Souvenir, 1855-1905* (London, 1905), *per* JCGB) Although later churchwarden of St George's, Bloomsbury, member of council of Whitefield's Tabernacle. One of vice-presidents of Bloomsbury Men's Meeting. (*CW*, 10 Oct. 1912, p. 3).

WWW 1916-1928. *WWBMP* 2.

THOMAS ROWLEY HILL
1 Mar. 1816 - 9 Oct. 1896
MP (L) for Worcester, 1874-85

Vinegar and wine manufacturer; of Hill, Evans and Co., Worcester (nowhere stated, but can be inferred from his marrying Mary, daughter of Edward Evans of Worcester). University College, London. Alderman of Worcester; sheriff, 1857; mayor, 1858. High Sheriff of Worcestershire, 1870. Contested Worcester, 1868, 1885 and 1886. Supported amendment of land laws (1885). JP, DL. Founded almshouses for four elderly women in Worcester. Of St Catherine's Hill, Worcester.

Member of Angel Street Congregational Church, Worcester, from 1834 and deacon "for more than twenty years", supporting Congregational work in the county. Hill was "earnestly attached to the doctrines and polity of the

churches with which he has a lifelong connection". (*Congregationalist*, Sept. 1879, pp. 705-7, quoted at pp. 705, 707). On committee of Congregational Union by 1870 (*CYB*, 1870, p. ix).
WWBMP. Boase. *T*, 10 Oct. 1896, p. 9.

Sir EDWARD THOMAS HOLDEN
1831 - 13 Nov. 1926
MP (L) for Walsall, Aug. 1891-92

Currier. Aldridge Grammar School. Member of Walsall town council 60 years; first freeman, alderman and twice mayor. Twice chairman of School Board. JP. Chairman of Walsall Liberal Association. Supported advanced Liberal programme (1892). Defeated at Walsall, 1892. Knight, 1907. Of Glenelg, Great Barr, near Walsall.

Member of Wednesbury Road Congregational Church, Walsall, from its foundation in 1857; deacon and Sunday school teacher (*CW*, 14 Nov. 1907, p. 3).
WWBMP 2.

ALFRED EDDISON HUTTON
1865 - 30 May 1947
MP (L) for Yorkshire, West Riding, S, Morley, 1892 - Jan. 1910

Manufacturer. Mill Hill School; Trinity College, Cambridge. Temporary chairman of committees, 1907-09. Of Crow Trees, Rawdon, Yorks.

Member of Eccleshill Congregational Church, Bradford (JCGB). Christian Endeavour worker. Treasurer, Yorkshire United College. (Surman) On Congregational Union committee (*CYB*, 1895, p. xiii). As chairman of Yorkshire Congregational Union, 1904, quoted Bentham: "If you would gain mankind, the best way is to appear to love them; and the best way of appearing to love them is to love them in reality" (Francis Wrigley, *The History of the Yorkshire Congregational Union: A Story of Fifty Years, 1873-1923* (London, n.d.), p. 119).
WWW 1941-50. *WWBMP* 2.

Sir DAVID BRYNMOR JONES
12 May 1852 - 6 Aug. 1921
MP (L) for Stroud, 1892-95
Swansea District, 1895-1914

Barrister. University College School and College, London. Called to bar, Middle Temple, 1876; bencher, 1899; reader, 1911. QC, 1893. Judge of county courts, 1885-92. Recorder of Merthyr Tydfil, 1910-14. Knight, 1906. PC, 1912. Hon. LLD, Wales, 1919. JP. Master in Lunacy from 1914. Member, Welsh Land Commission, 1893-96. Chairman, County Court Departmental Committees, 1893 and 1899. Imperialist in Boer War (Morgan, p. 179). Chairman, Metropolitan Police Commission, 1906. Proposed Welsh National Council with educational and other powers, 1906 (Morgan, p. 223). Member, Welsh Church Commission, 1907. Chairman, Welsh Parliamentary Party, 1910-14. Member, Venereal Disease Commission, 1913. Recorder of Cardiff, 1914-15. Member of court of referees, 1896-1914. A chairman of standing committees in Commons, 1906-14. Hon. counsel and member of court, University of Wales. Vice-president and chairman of council, Cymmrodorion Society. Published *Essay on Home Rule and Imperial Sovereignty* (1886), *Address on Welsh History in the Light of Recent Research* (1891) and (with Principal Sir John Rhys) *The Welsh People* (1900). Contributed to transactions of the Cymmrodorion Society on mediaeval Wales. Of 27 Bryanston Square, London.

Son of Thomas Jones, Independent minister, chairman of Congregational Union of England and Wales, 1871-72. Edited his father's *The Divine Order and Other Sermons* with preface by Robert Browning (1884). Married Florence, widow of A. de M. Mocatta and daughter of Major Lionel Cohen, 1892, which casts some doubt on his Congregational allegiance. Yet passive resister.

DWB. WWW 1916-1928. *WWBMP* 2. Surman.

Sir JOHN JONES-JENKINS
10 May 1835 - 27 July 1915
MP (L) for Carmarthen District, Jan. 1882-86
(LU) for Carmarthen District, 1895-1900

Proprietor, Beaufort Tinplate Works and Cwmfelin Tinplate and Steel Works. Chief proprietor, Mumbles Railway Co. Chairman, Tirdonkin Collieries Ltd; Swansea Dock and Railway co.; Rhondda and Swansea Bay Railway Co. Founder, Swansea Bank. Director, National Accident Insurance Co. Ltd; North British and Mercantile Insurance Co.; Metropolitan Bank; Midland Bank. Chairman, Swansea Harbour Trust, 1891-98. First president, Swansea Metal Exchange. Swansea councillor from 1865; mayor, 1869-70, 1879-80, 1880-81. Glamorgan county councillor from 1888; High Sheriff, 1889. Freeman of Swansea, 1895. JP, DL. Knight, 1881. Baron Glantawe, June 1906. Contested Carmarthen District as L, 1880. Unsuccessful LU candidate there, 1886, 1892, 1900. Member of Loyal and Patriotic Union, 1886. Rejoined Liberals, 1905. Hon.

lieutenant, Royal Naval Artillery Volunteers. President, Royal Institution of Wales, 1889-90. Patron, Oddfellows. Member of governing body for intermediate and technical education, Swansea. Of 43 Pall Mall, London, and The Grange, Swansea.

Member of a Welsh Independent chapel, then of Walter Road Congregational Church, Swansea. Afterwards became Anglican. (Information from the Rev. I. T. Rees)

WWBMP 2.

JAMES KERSHAW
1795 - 27 Apr. 1864
MP (L) for Stockport, Dec. 1847 - Apr. 1864

Cotton manufacturer and calico printer; partner of Kershaw, Lees and Sidebottom. His Mersey Mills in Stockport employed 1,200 in 1842. Obtained municipal franchise for Manchester, 1838. Alderman of Manchester; mayor, 1842-43. Member of Anti-Corn Law League committee, 1838. Supported South in American Civil War. Favoured ballot, short parliaments, repeal of ratepayer clauses of 1832 Reform Act, repeal of game laws; opposed all religious endowments (1864). Of Manor House, Streatham, Surrey.

Deacon of Mosley Street Congregational Chapel, Manchester, under Dr Halley, remaining so when church moved to Cavendish Street (JCGB). Regular chairman of LMS meetings.

WWBMP. Boase. Not in *LN.*

BATTY LANGLEY
1834 - 17 Feb. 1914
MP (L) for Sheffield, Attercliffe, July 1894 - Apr. 1909

Timber merchant. On Sheffield council 36 years, becoming alderman. As mayor, 1893, promoted conference to settle coal strike. Chairman of Sheffield Burial Board. JP. President of Sheffield Liberal Association. First president, National Association of General Railway Clerks, formed in Sheffield,1897-98. Retired to Queen's Park, Bournemouth.

Teacher and secretary of Uppingham Congregational Sunday school (*Sheffield Daily Independent*, 18 Feb. 1914). Member of Queen Street Congregational Church, Sheffield, from 1852, deacon (1861) and church secretary. Chairman, Sheffield Congregational Association, 1879. Trustee of Memorial Hall. (Surman; *BW*, 5 Mar. 1914, p. 657). Member, Congregational Union committee (*CYB*, 1885, p. xvii). Chairman, Yorkshire Congregational Union, 1896, when he opined that if the Union of

Christendom could be realised, "it would only be a cradle in which to rock to sleep the activities of the church" (Francis Wrigley, *The History of the Yorkshire Congregational Union: A Story of Fifty Years, 1873-1923* (London, n.d.), p. 116). Sunday school teacher, secretary and superintendent (*CW*, 19 Feb. 1914, p. 2). Promoted Sunday School Union Montgomery Hall scheme (*Sheffield Daily Independent*, 18 Feb. 1914). President of Sheffield Sunday School Union.

WWW 1897-1916. *WWBMP* 2.

Sir THOMAS LEA
  17 Jan. 1838 - 9 Jan. 1902
  MP (L) for Kidderminster, 1868-74
  Co. Donegal, Dec. 1879-85
  MP (LU) for Londonderry, S, 1886-1900

Ironfounder. Chairman of Birmingham banking firm. Defeated at Kidderminster, 1874; Donegal, Aug. 1876; Donegal, E, 1885. Bart, 1892. JP. County cricketer for Worcestershire and other counties. Of The Larches, Kidderminster.

Member of Baxter Congregational Church, Kidderminster? Only Congregational Unionist at 1892 general election (F. H. Stead to W. E. Gladstone, 1 July 1892, Gladstone Papers, BL Add. MS 44515, f. 82).

WWW 1897-1916. *WWBMP* 2.

HENRY LEE
  1817-1904
  MP (L) for Southampton, 1880-85

Merchant and manufacturer. Director of Manchester Chamber of Commerce. JP. Favoured redistribution of seats and amendment of land laws (1885). Unsuccessful candidate at Salford, 1874; Southampton, 1885; and Manchester, NW, 1886. Chairman of Triennial Conference of Liberation Society, 1892 (*CW*, 5 May 1892). "The first impression he gives is of robustness of character . . ." (*Congregationalist,* Dec. 1880, p. 971). Of Sedgley Park, Prestwich, Lancs.

Son of a founder of Hollinshead Street Congregational Chapel, Chorley, Lancs (*LN*, vol. 2, p. 23). Member of Chapel Street Chapel, Salford, for a long time, next one of founders of Richmond Congregational Church, Salford, and then leader in creation of Broughton Park Congregational Church, Salford (*Congregationalist* , Dec. 1880, p. 972); member from 1875, treasurer to 1881, deacon to 1882 (JCGB). On executive committee of Lancashire Congregational Union (*Congregationalist*, De 1880, p. 972).

Treasurer, Lancashire Independent College, 1870-78 (Joseph Thompson, *Lancashire Independent College, 1843-1893* (Manchester, 1893), p. 200). Supported formation of Lancashire and Cheshire Chapel and School Building Society, 1868. Trustee of Woodward Trust for ministers of small churches from 1870. Established minimum salary for evangelists (£100) and ministers (£150) of Lancashire Congregational Union, 1874. (B. Nightingale, *The Story of the Lancashire Congregational Union* (Manchester, 1906), pp. 97, 102, 110). Trustee of Memorial Hall from 1872 (Surman). On committee of Congregational Union by 1874 and, though there were gaps, still there in 1898 (*CYB*, 1874, p. xv; 1898, p. xiii). Supporter of LMS. Visited Australia with Alexander Hannay on behalf of Colonial Missionary Society. Promoter of idea, and first treasurer, of Congregational Church Aid Society, 1879-92. (Peel, pp. 294, 303, 306, 308). Travelled to Egypt and Holy Land, 1872, and to N America, 1877, with R. W. Dale, a close friend (A. W. W. Dale, *The Life of R. W. Dale of Birmingham* (London, 1898), pp. 308-10, 332). Chairman of Free Church Congress, 1892 (*CW,* 14 Jan. 1892, p. 28). Willing to contribute to parish churches (*Congregationalist*, Dec. 1880, pp. 972-3).

WWBMP. Congregationalist, Dec. 1880, pp. 969-73.

GEORGE LEEMAN
22 Aug. 1809 - 25 Feb. 1882
MP (L) for York, 1865-68, Feb. 1871-80

Solicitor, partner in Leeman, Wilkinson and Leeman of York. Chairman of North Eastern Railway, 1874-80. Had interests in cotton spinning and iron works. Councillor, alderman from 1850 and three times Lord Mayor of York, 1853, 1860 and 1870. JP, DL. Clerk of the peace for the E Riding until death. Appeared in court in 1827 to defend church rates protestors and in 1837 tried to persuade corporation to support petition against church rates. Supported secret ballot from 1835. Favoured free trade, but did not identify with Anti-Corn Law League because of habitual caution. Undisputed leader of York Liberals from 1862. Initially candidate for parliament in 1852, but withdrew in favour of W. M. E. Milner and Henry Vincent. Supported Lord's Day Defence Association, 1850s. Whiggish over parliamentary reform by 1857. Second most important York citizen of the nineteenth century after George Hudson, the "railway king". Of The Mount, York.

Member of Salem Congregational Church, York, under James Parsons, from 1833, becoming deacon. Known as "the deacon of Salem" to Tory opponents. (Peacock, p. 235). On committee of Congregational Union by 1870 (*CYB*, 1870, p. ix). Second wife was Ellen, widow of the Rev. Charles

Payton of York. Attended Priory Street Baptist Church during ministry of F. B. Meyer (Ian Randall).

Alf Peacock, "George Leeman and York Politics, 1833-80", in Charles Feinstein(ed.), *York, 1831-1981* (York, 1981), pp. 234-54. *WWBMP.* Boase. Papers at National Archives.

JOSEPH JOHNSON LEEMAN
1842 - 2 Nov. 1883
MP (L) for York, 1880 - Nov. 1883

Solicitor, partner in Leeman, Wilkinson and Leeman. Son of George Leeman. St Peter's School, York. DL. Of Acomb Priory, York.

Presumably member of Salem Congregational Church, York.

WWBMP. Boase.

Sir JOSEPH LEIGH
1841 - 22 Sept. 1908
MP (L) for Stockport, 1892-95, 1900-06

Cotton manufacturer. Director of Manchester Ship Canal. Stockport Grammar School. Councillor from 1875 and four times mayor of Stockport, 1884, 1886-88. Unsuccessful candidate at Stockport, 1885, 1886, 1895. Freeman of Stockport. Founder (1897) of Stockport Technical School, to which he contributed £3,500. JP. Knight, 1894. Chevalier of the Legion of Honour. Favoured old age pensions, better housing for the poor, rating of land values, temperance, administrative reform in War Office (1905). Of The Towers, Didsbury.

Congregationalist (*CW*, 18 July 1895, p. 588).

WWBMP 2.

Sir JOHN LENG
10 Apr. 1828 - 13 Dec. 1906
MP (L) for Dundee, Sept. 1889-1905

Newspaper proprietor. Chairman from 1893 of Donside Paper Mills. Son of Adam Leng of Hull. Hull Grammar School. Sub-editor of *Hull Advertiser* (1847) and editor of *Dundee Advertiser* (1851). Established popular periodicals in Scotland including *The People's Journal* (1858) and *The People's Friend* (1869). Pioneered illustration in daily newspapers. Author of *America in 1876*, *Scotch Banking Reform* (1881), *American Competition with British Agriculture* (1881), *Practical Politics* (1885), *The Best Methods of Dealing with the Unemployed* (1886), *Home Rule All*

Round (1890), *Letters from India and Ceylon* (1896), etc. LLD, St Andrews, 1904. JP, DL. Knight, 1893. In 1864 inspired formation of Dundee Working Men's Association (Michael St John, *The Demands of the People: Dundee Radicalism, 1850-1870* (Dundee, 1997), p. 13). Favoured temperance, taxation of land values, registration reform (1905); "his belief in progress remained firm to the last" (*Dundee Advertiser*, 13 Dec. 1906, quoted by *ODNB*). Of Kinbrae, Newport, Fife.

Senior deacon of Newport, Fife, Congregational Church (*CW*, 9 Feb. 1905, p. 3).

ODNB (omitting religion). *WWBMP* 2. *WWW* 1897-1916. Papers at Dundee Central Library.

THOMAS RICHMOND LEUTY
1853 - 15 Apr. 1911
MP (L) for Leeds, E, Apr. 1895-1900

Linen manufacturer, Castleton Mills, Leeds. Bramham College. Leeds town councillor from 1882; mayor, 1893-94. Favoured Newcastle Programme, limitation of powers of Lords, eight hours for miners (1900). Unsuccessful candidate for Leeds, N, 1892. Married, 1880, Annie, daughter of John Arthington, donor to missionary societies. Of Headingley Lodge, Leeds.

Member of East Parade Congregational Church, Leeds, until transferred, 1871, to Headingley Hill Congregational Church (JCGB). President of Leeds Free Church Council (*CW*, 9 May 1895).

WWBMP 2.

WALTER STOWE BRIGHT McLAREN
17 Apr. 1853 - 29 June 1912
MP (L) for Cheshire, Crewe, 1886-95, Apr. 1910 - June 1912

Worsted spinner in Keighley until retired, 1890. Director of coal and iron companies, including Bolckow, Vaughan and Co. Son of Duncan Mclaren MP and Priscilla, sister of John Bright. Craigmount School, Edinburgh, and Edinburgh University. Edited *The Electioneer* before Keighley School Board election, 1875. On executive of Manchester Society for Women's Suffrage, 1884-95, on executive of National Society for Women's Suffrage from 1888 and on executive of Men's League for Women's Suffrage, becoming vice-president, 1907. Wife, known as Mrs Eva McLaren, equally active. Opposed state regulation of prostitution in India. Member of a peace society in London. Supported industrial conciliation. Favoured disestablishment, women's suffrage and free trade (1912). Of 56 Ashley Gardens, SW, and Great Comp Cottage, Borough Green.

Congregationalist (*BW*, 18 May 1888, p. 50).

ODNB. WWW 1897-1916. *WWBMP* 2. *T*, 2 July 1912.

PETER STEWART MacLIVER
1820 - 19 Apr. 1891
MP (L) for Plymouth, 1880-85

Proprietor of *Western Daily Press,* founded in 1858, the first daily newspaper in the western counties (J. R. Grant, *The Newspaper Press: Its Origin, Progress and Present Prospects*, 3 vols (London, 1871), vol. 3, p. 270), of *Bristol Observer,* founded 1859, weekly, as "a family paper in the strict sense of the word" (Grant, vol. 3, p. 271) and of *Bristol Evening News* (1877). Glasgow High School and University. Served on *Tyne Mercury,* 1845, then editing *Newcastle Guardian.* Contested Plymouth, 1885; Glasgow, St Rollox, 1886. JP. Advocate of cause of Post Office officials. Of Ardnave, Weston-super-Mare, Somerset.

On Congregational Union committee (*Congregationalist*).

WWBMP. Boase. *Congregationalist*, Dec. 1881, pp. 977-82 (without reference to church membership).

JOHN GORDON McMINNIES
1817 - 1 Feb. 1890
MP (L) for Warrington, 1880-85

Cotton manufacturer; senior partner in W. Bashall and Co. Owner of Farington Mill, near Preston. Alderman of Warrington. JP. Of Farington Lodge and Summer House, Warrington.

A key figure in foundation of Wycliffe Congregational Church, Warrington, "who always displayed deep interest in and strong attachment to Wycliffe" (*The Wycliffe Church Record*, 101 (Oct. 1898), p. 3, *per* JCGB).

WWBMP. Boase. Not in *LN.*

HUGH MASON
30 Jan. 1817 - 2 Feb. 1886
MP (L) for Ashton-under-Lyne, 1880-85

Cotton manufacturer and merchant. A founder of the Cotton Supply Association, 1857. Chairman of executive, Manchester Cotton Association, begun 1860. President of Cotton Spinners' Association, 1861. Vice-president of Steam Users' Association from 1864; president from 1875. President of Society for the Promotion of Scientific Industry, 1875. A director of Manchester Chamber of Commerce, 1864; vice-president, 1871; president, 1871-74. Established New Oxford colony as estate for his workpeople, providing in 1861 library, lecture hall, reading room and smoking room. Every year there was a winter programme of "lectures, concerts, and elevating entertainments" (*Congregationalist*, Oct. 1880, p. 794). Enlarged lecture hall in 1868, adding picture gallery and baths. He considered they were "brothers and sisters in that Oxford colony – working together for one common end – the mutual welfare of the workpeople and the employer" (quoted by Bowman, p. 462). No strike ever took place at his mills. Provided recreation ground, 1870. Introduced Saturday half-holiday in 1871 to displeasure of other employers. Member of Ashton-under-Lyne town council from 1856; alderman, 1866-74; mayor, 1858-60. Two Russian guns captured in the Crimean War were placed on steps of Town Hall, but, according to Mason, "there is no act of my Mayoralty on which I look back with deeper regret than that I had the slightest hand in bringing those wretched instruments of destruction to the front of our Town Hall" (Bowman, p. 463). JP, DL. As JP, 1863, caused mob of rioters to disperse. Supported Ashton Mechanics' Institute from start in 1839 and sometime secretary. Supported opening of public library, giving 1,000 volumes, 1882. Established *Ashton News*, 1868-74. Life Governor of Owens College, Manchester, 1870. Supported movement for public park, 1856-57, but disapproved its site in Stalybridge. Active in erecting Ashton District Infirmary, 1861. Founder of Cobden Club and Manchester Reform Club, 1866. Member of Mersey Docks and Harbour Board from 1872. Vice-chairman from 1861 of S Lancashire Registration Association. (Bowman, p. 464). Seconded address at opening of 1880 session. Carried Boilers Explosion Bill, 1882. Secured National Liberal Federation for Ashton, 1882. Defeated at Ashton, 1885. Supported North in American Civil War, relieving distress during cotton famine. Opposed Ballot Act as "un-English" (Bowman, p. 646n). Active in Liberation Society. President of Manchester and Salford Temperance Union and Band of Hope Union. Vice-president of United Kingdom Alliance, 1875. As MP, secured passage of Local Option Bill, 1880. Wrote *On the Use of Tobacco* (1885) against smoking. From 1881 until 1884 leader of women's suffrage group in Commons, though opposed enfranchising married women and did not insist on feminist amendment to 1884 Reform Bill (Harrison, p. 86). Interested in Lancashire dialect literature. Photograph shows strong, shaven, projecting chin. According to W. H. Mills, *The Manchester Reform Club, 1817-1921* (Manchester, 1922), p. 10, "either one belonged to that half of society which accounted him as little less than deity or to the other half of society which stoned his carriage windows". Formerly Methodist New Connexion Sunday school teacher, taking class in branch school at Waterloo among colliers (Bowman, p. 461). Member of Albion Chapel, Ashton-under-Lyne, from 1846; treasurer, 1858; deacon, 1860-86; Sunday school teacher. Presided over construction of Albion Sunday school, 1861-62. As MP attended Grafton Square Congregational Church, Clapham. (J. Guinness Rogers, *Autobiography,* pp. 112-14). Supported LMS, BFBS. Bought cottages as site for Charlestown Congregational Chapel and schools, whose foundation stone he laid, Aug. 1866. Laid foundation stone of Lees Street Congregational school chapel, 22 Apr. 1871. With Nathaniel Buckley, bought Dukinfield Old Hall chapel for new church, 1872. (*LN*, vol. 5, pp. 304, 63, 313). "He is too pronounced in his opinions, and too outspoken in the advocacy of them, not to have many critics and opponents." The union of the devout Christian worker and the robust Liberal politician creates "a masculine type of piety worthy of all honour". (*Congregationalist*, Oct. 1880, pp. 796, 797).

Winifred M. Bowman, *England in Ashton-under-Lyne* (Altrincham, 1960), pp. 459-64. *ODNB* (good on religion). Brian Harrison, *Dictionary of British Temperance Biography* (Coventry, 1973), p. 86. *Congregationalist*, Oct. 1880, pp. 793-7; Mar. 1886, pp. 224-30. J. C. G. Binfield, "The Dynamic of Grandeur: Albion Church, Ashton-under-Lyne", *Transactions of the Lancashire and Cheshire Antiquarian Society* 85 (1988), 173-92.

EDWARD MIALL

8 May 1809 - 29 Apr. 1881
MP (L) for Rochdale, 1852-57
Bradford, Mar. 1869-74

Minister and disestablishment agitator. Schoolteacher from age of sixteen. Wymondley College, near Stevenage, Herts. In pastorate at Ware, Herts (1831-34), and Bond Street, Leicester (1835-39). Formed Voluntary Church Society, actively opposing church rates. Editor, the *Nonconformist*, 1841-77. In 1844 organised Dissenting convention that formed the British Anti-State Church Association, which in 1853 became the Liberation Society. Promoter of peace congresses, 1848-53. Contested Southwark, Sept. 1845; Halifax, 1847; Rochdale, 1857; Banbury, 1859; Bradford, 1868. Author of *The British Churches in Relation to the British People* (1849), *Bases of Belief* (1853), *Politics of Christianity* (1863), *An Editor Off the Line* (1865) and *The Title Deeds of the Church of England to he Parochial Endowments* (1862). On Newcastle Commission on popular education, 1858-61. Proposed English disestablishment in Commons,

9 May 1871. Advocate of voluntary moral limits on commercial gain and labour exchanges. Working in the capital from 1841, he lived in Stoke Newington, Tottenham, Holloway, Upper Norwood, Forest Hill and Sevenoaks.

Membership after move to London not found. Usually attended only morning services, hearing Congregational and Baptist ministers. Deeply interested in the idiosyncratic S. A. Tipple of Upper Norwood and respected Alexander Maclaren. (Miall, p. 359).

Arthur Miall, *Life of Edward Miall* (London, 1884). Clyde Binfield, "Pacemaker or Crotcheteer?: The Impact of a Strolling Agitator: A Study of Edward Miall", *So Down to Prayers* (London, 1977), chap. 5. *ODNB. BDMBR* 2. *WWBMP.*

ROBERT MILLIGAN
10 Oct. 1786 - 1 July 1862
MP (L) for Bradford, Oct. 1851-57

Worsted merchant; senior partner in Milligan, Forbes and Co. Moved, penniless, from Dunnance, Kirkcudbright to Yorkshire, *c.* 1802, and by 1810 draper in Bradford (http://www.bradfordhistorical.org.uk//antiquary/third/vol03/milligan.html). Became alderman and as first mayor (1847-48), suppressed Chartist disorder (Koditschek, pp. 560-1). JP. Member of council of Anti-Corn Law League. Favoured franchise extension, increase of direct taxation and ballot (1857). Supported Mechanics' Institute, 1832. A founder of *Bradford Observer*, 1834. Chairman of Bradford Caledonian Society, 1836. Gave annual feast to workers to encourage morale (Koditschek, pp. 310, 297, 325, 425). Of Acacia House, Rawdon.

Pewholder at Horton Lane Chapel, Bradford. Sunday school teacher there (http://education.bradfordcollege.ac.uk/nutter1.htm). Attended Salem Chapel, Bradford, from its foundation in 1835 (first website: vol02/Brunswick.html). Builder of Rawdon Congregational Church (JCGB). According to Dr Benjamin Godwin, a retired Baptist minister, at his funeral, "though not distinguished by eloquence he was always at his post as a man of business.... It is only within these last few years that, while attending to his parliamentary duties, he took the decided step of joining a Christian church.... Of his own feelings in religious matters of a personal kind he spoke sparingly." (*Bradford Observer*, 10 July 1862, p. 6).

WWBMP. Boase. Theodore Koditschek, *Class Formation and Urban-Industrial Society: Bradford, 1750-1850* (Cambridge, 1990). *Bradford Observer*, 3 July 1862, p. 5.

JOHN REMINGTON MILLS

15 Jan. 1798 - 22 Nov. 1879

MP (L) for Wycombe, Mar. 1862-68

Silk manufacturer, retiring in 1840. On council of University College, London, 1836-44. Deputy chairman of Religious Freedom Society, 1839. Treasurer (1836-44) and chairman (1844-53) of Dissenting Deputies (Manning, p 485). Member of Central Anti-Maynooth Committee, 1845. JP. Contested Leeds, Mar. and June 1857; Finsbury, Dec. 1861; Wycombe, 1868. Favoured ballot and abolition of church rates (1867). Brother of Thomas Mills, MP for Totnes, 1852-62, and brother-in-law of Charles Trueman, MP for Helston, 1857-59. President of Orphan Working School, Haverstock Hill. Owned land, specially at Clermont, Norfolk. Patron of one living. FRGS. Died a millionaire. Of Kingswood Lodge, Englefield Green, Surrey (1867), and later of Kingswood Lodge, Tunbridge Wells.

Member of King's Weigh House from 1821 (Church records, Dr Williams's Library), transferring to Chase Side, Enfield, and then to Harecourt, Islington. Founder of Egham Hill Congregational Chapel, 1851, and benefactor of Tunbridge Wells Congregational Chapel. (JCGB) On provisional committee of Congregational Union, 1831; trustee from 1836. Treasurer of Colonial Missionary Society from 1836. Supported Pastors' Insurance Aid Society from 1853. Presided at Congregational Commemoration of Great Ejection, 1862, and at opening of Memorial Hall, 1875, having contributed £12,000. (Peel, pp. 49, 95, 98, 208, 240, 277). Most generous donor to Congregational Chapel Building Society from 1853. Nephew of Thomas Wilson, another Congregational silk manufacturer and benefactor.

BDMBR 2 (JCGB). *WWBMP.* Boase.

JOHN LLOYD MORGAN

13 Feb. 1861 - 17 May 1944

MP (L) for Carmarthenshire, July 1889 - Nov. 1910

Barrister. Tettenhall College; Owens College, Manchester; Trinity Hall, Cambridge. Called to bar, Inner Temple, 1884. KC, 1906. Recorder of Swansea, 1908-10. Carmarthen County Court Judge, 1910-26. Of 105 Pall Mall, London.

Son of William Morgan, Independent minister of Carmarthen Presbyterian College, whose life he published (1886). Perhaps member of English Congregational Church, Carmarthen, where father had been minister. Personal member, Congregational Union. (Surman)

WW 1920. *WWBMP* 2.

SAMUEL MORLEY

15 Oct. 1809 - 5 Sept. 1886
MP (L) for Nottingham, 1865-66 (unseated on petition)
Bristol, 1868-85

Hosiery manufacturer; head of I. and R. Morley of Nottingham and London, relinquishing control in 1878. By 1886, firm had 7 Midland factories with 3,000 direct employees. London warehouse equipped with reading rooms and parlours. School of William Carver, Independent minister, at Melbourn, Cambs; Buller's School, Southampton. Received medal commemorating repeal of Test and Corporation Acts in 1828. Opponent of church rates in 1830s. Treasurer of Congregational fund to fight Graham's education proposals, 1843. Early supporter of Anti-State Church Association. Chairman of Dissenters' Parliamentary Committee, 1847. Chairman of electoral committee of Liberation Society, 1855. Member and chairman of parliamentary committee of Dissenting Deputies. Chairman of City committee of Administrative Reform Association, 1855-56. Chairman of Bank Act and Currency Reform Association from 1861. Donor to National Reform Union and Reform League. Withdrew from Liberation Society executive, 1868. Major proprietor of *Daily News*, 1868. Defeated at Bristol, Apr.1868. In 1869 shared platform with Karl Marx in support of proposed Trade Union Bill. Seconded address to the throne, 9 Feb. 1871. Chaired meeting at Cannon Street Hotel, 1872, for trade union leaders and radicals. Supported *Beehive, Commonwealth* and National Agricultural Labourers' Union. Director of Artisans', Labourers' and General Dwellings Company from 1877. Member of London School Board, 1870-76. Donor to Dissenting schools, Cavendish College, Cambridge, and university colleges at Bristol, Nottingham and Aberystwyth; and to *Eclectic Review, British Quarterly Review* and *Contemporary Review*. Supported temperance, local veto and Blue Ribbon movement. Published *Drinking Usages of the Commercial Room* (1862). Piloted bill prohibiting payment of wages in public houses through Commons, 1881. Supported sabbath enforcement; vice-president of Working Men's Lord's Day Observance Society. Opposed contagious diseases acts. Opposed Bradlaugh in 1880s. Declined peerage, 1885. JP. Commissioner of lieutenancy for London. Millionaire and philanthropist, with giving estimated at £20-30,000 per annum. Gave interest-free loan to Lord Shaftesbury. Supported Royal College of Music from 1884. Became effectively terse speaker. According to J. C. Harrison, he was "remarkable for wholeheartedness", displaying the "sweetness and graciousness of his disposition" (pp. iv, 11). Of 18 Wood Street, Cheapside (warehouse); Craven Lodge, Stamford Hill, 1854-70; 16 Upper Brook Street, 1870s; 34 Grosvenor Street afterwards; and Hall Place, Leigh, near Tunbridge, Kent.

Member of Old Gravel Pit Chapel, Homerton, and treasurer of Homerton College. Transferred to St Thomas' Square Congregational Chapel, Hackney, becoming deacon. Gradual conversion completed under sermon of James Parsons. Transferred to King's Weigh House in 1836, where became close to Thomas Binney but declined to serve as deacon (Hodder, pp. 17,18, 20-1, 64-8; Clyde Binfield, *George Williams and the Y.M.C.A.* (London, 1973), p. 24). Treasurer of Congregational Home Missionary Society from 1858 (Hodder, p. 95); and co-treasurer of Church Aid and Home Mission Society from 1878. Spent £14,400 on new chapels, 1864-70, and £6,000 for Memorial Hall. On executive committee of YMCA from 1844, giving £500 towards London Association buying Exeter Hall, 1880. Gave to Bristol Cathedral and to Leigh parish church, where he was patron of the living from 1870. (*ODNB*) Declined chair of Congregational Union for 1886. Supported at least 11 Congregational theological colleges and Homerton Congregational Normal College. Treasurer of Ancient Merchants' Lectures, 1849-79. Supported theatre services from 1859, Lambeth Baths Mission from 1861 and lay evangelists. (*BDMBR* 2) In giving, "He was anxious for *results* – visible results. . . ." (Harrison, p. vii).

Edwin Hodder, *The Life of Samuel Morley* (London, 1887). J. C. Harrison, *Samuel Morley: Personal Reminiscences* (London, 1886). *ODNB* (good but not detailed on religion). *BDMBR* 2 (JCGB). *Congregationalist,* Jan. 1880, pp. 1-8. Letters and papers, Dr Williams's Library, London.

SAMUEL MOSS
13 Dec. 1858 - 14 May 1918
MP (L) for Denbighshire, E, Sept. 1897- June 1906

Barrister. Worcester College, Oxford. BCL, 1880. Called to bar, Lincoln's Inn, 1880. Chester and N Wales Circuit. Author of *English Land Laws* (1886). Alderman, vice-chairman then chairman of Denbighshire CC. Member of Chester town council. JP. Assistant boundary commissioner for Wales, 1887. Favoured disestablishment, ten hours, one man one vote and reform of Lords (1905). Passive resister. County court judge, 1906. Of 50 Hough Green, Chester, and Accre Hall, Llandegla, near Wrexham.

Congregationalist (*CW*, 28 June 1906, p. 3). Active Nonconformist (*BW*, 15 Feb. 1906, p. 538). Member of Northgate Street Congregational Chapel, Chester?

WWBMP 2. *WWW* 1916-1928.

Sir MARK OLDROYD
30 May 1843 - 5 July 1927
MP (L) for Dewsbury, Nov. 1886 - Jan. 1901

Woollen manufacturer and colliery proprietor; chairman, Mark Oldroyd and Sons. In 1888 four large factories in Dewsbury produced 7-8,000 yards of heavy broad cloth a day, employing 2,000. Director of Airedale Collieries Ltd, Castleford. President of Heavy Woollen District Manufacturers' Association, 1912-18. Dewsbury Grammar School, Batley Grammar School. Councillor (1868-71, 1884-85), alderman (from 1885) and mayor (1887-88) of Dewsbury. First hon. freeman of Dewsbury, 1919. JP. Knight, 1909. First chairman of Non-County Boroughs Association. Supported West Riding Free Trade Federation. President of Dewsbury Central Liberal Association, 1886. Favoured one man one vote, payment of MPs, land reform and local veto (1892); undenominational education, disestablishment and reform of land laws (1901). During 1892 election, the Tory *Dewsbury Chronicle* ran a series of articles under the title "The Gospel according to St. Mark". 1900, urged suppression of "such doings and teachings as are subversive of the Protestant foundation of the Church of England". His Conservative opponent compared Oldroyd to Pliable in *Pilgrim's Progress* because of his flexibility on so many issues, such as favouring annexation of the Boer republics but their self-government (James, pp. 114, 128, 129, 127). Married, 1871, Maria Mewburn, sister of wife of R. W. Perks, later Wesleyan MP. Supported local Guild of Help and Dewsbury Day Nursery. Gave £10,000 to Dewsbury and District Infirmary for children's ward, 1919. Of Hyrstlands, Dewsbury.

Member for sixty-three years, senior deacon and treasurer of United Congregational Church, Dewsbury (*ODNB*). Entered New College, London, with a view to ministry (*BW*, 6 Apr. 1911, p. 5), but left to enter family firm (*ODNB*). Returned home to conduct men's Bible class each Sunday while MP (*CW*, 1 July 1909, p. 2). Addressed Congregational Union annual meetings and supported missionary work (*ODNB*). Member of Congregational Union committee from 1892; still there, 1900 (*CYB*, 1892, p. xix; 1900, p. xii).

C. J. James, *M.P. for Dewsbury* (Brighouse, Yorks, 1970). *ODNB. WWW* 1916-1928.

JOHN DICK PEDDIE

1824 - 12 Mar. 1891

MP (L) for Kilmarnock District, 1880-85

Architect, retiring 1878. Son of James Peddie, WS. Born in Edinburgh. Edinburgh University. Studied law for five years before becoming architect, designing Queen Street Hall, Edinburgh, etc. Associate of the Royal Scottish Academy, 1870; member of council; secretary, 1870-76.

Edinburgh School Board for 3 years. On council of Edinburgh University. Introduced disestablishment resolutions in Commons. Defeated at Kilmarnock, 1885. United disestablishment movement in Scotland, 1886, effectively excluding Liberation Society. Of 33 Buckingham Terrace, Edinburgh.

Congregationalist (*BW*, 18 May 1888, p. 50).

WWBMP. Boase. *Scotsman,* 13 Mar. 1891, p. 5 (omitting religious allegiance).

APSLEY PELLATT
27 Nov. 1791 - 17 Apr. 1863
MP (L) for Southwark, 1852-57

Glass manufacturer at Falcon Glassworks, Southwark. Took out patent for glass incrustation, 1819, and later patents. Rediscovered art of making crackle glass for which Venice famous. Common councillor, City of London, for seven years, successfully campaigning for admission of Jews as freemen. Gave evidence to Commons select committee on Sunday observance with reference to Farringdon market, 1832. Summoned for refusal of church rate, mid-1830s, defending himself in person. Vice-chairman (1853-56) and chairman (1855-63) of Dissenting Deputies (Manning, p. 485). "Though not conspicuous as a speaker, nor gifted with the qualities of a statesman", one of the distinct Nonconformist party in Commons (*Nonconformist,* 22 Apr. 1863, p. 309). Introduced bill to facilitate Dissenters' marriages, 1854, 1855 and 1856. Secured modification of distinction between consecrated and unconsecrated ground in public cemeteries, 1857. Secured act to define law on crossed cheques, 1856. Favoured household suffrage, equal electoral districts, no property qualifications, ballot and short parliaments; opposed state endowment of religion and therefore Maynooth grant (1856). Unsuccessful candidate for Bristol, 1847; Southwark, 1857 and 1859. Voted against Palmerston over Chinese war, 1857, costing him his seat. Commissioner for Great Exhibition, 1851, and juror for 1862 exhibition. On council of Institute of Civil Engineers from 1840, and of School of Design. Favoured improving Southwark drainage. Supported British Orphan School, London Female Penitentiary. Published *Memoir on the Origin, Progress and Improvement of Glass Manufactures* (1821), expanded as *Curiosities of Glass Making* (1849); and *Brief Memoir of the Jews* (1826). Fellow of genealogical and historical societies. Living at Staines, Middlesex, from 1843, established model farm. Also of Holland Street, London.

Deacon of Fetter Lane Independent Chapel, London. Member of

provisional committee of Congregational Union, 1831 (Peel, p. 49). Member of Staines Congregational Chapel for 20 years and treasurer, SW Middlesex Congregational Association. Laid foundation stone of Folkestone Congregational Chapel, 18 Aug. 1857 (Thomas Timpson, *Church History of Kent* (London, 1859), p. 513). "Open-handed generosity was one of the most marked features of his character. . . . a true Christian gentleman of great shrewdness and amiability" (*Nonconformist*, 22 Apr. 1863, p. 309).

ODNB. Boase. *Evangelical Magazine*, June 1863, pp. 394-5 (reproducing next, adding only funeral). *Nonconformist*, 22 Apr. 1863, p. 309.

JAMES PILKINGTON
1804 - 17 Feb. 1890
MP (L) for Blackburn, 1847-65

Cotton manufacturer of Park Place Mill, Blackburn. Director of Lancashire and Yorkshire Railway. Opened Park Road British School, 1851. Favoured ballot, redistribution of seats; opposed to all religious endowments (1865). Defeated at Blackburn, 1865. JP, DL. Survived being garrotted and robbed in London, 15 July 1862. Bought Swinethwaite Hall, west of West Witton, 1849. Also of Park Place House, Blackburn.

Of Park Road Congregational Chapel, Blackburn (Patrick Joyce, "The Factory Politics of Lancashire in the Later Nineteenth Century", *Historical Journal* 18 (1975), p. 537), which was founded in 1852 and had its building erected in 1858.

WWBMP. Boase. *T,* 20 Feb. 1890, p. 1.

RICHARD PILKINGTON
1841 - 12 Mar. 1908
MP (C) for Lancashire, Newton, Jan. 1899-1906

Glass manufacturer; partner of Pilkington Brothers. Four times mayor of St Helens, 1881, 1896-98. Defeated at Newton, 1906. JP. Colonel in charge of 2nd Volunteer Battalion, Prince of Wales S Lancashire Regiment. Of Rainford Hall, St Helens, Lancs.

Member, deacon and Sunday school teacher at Ormskirk Street Congregational Church, St Helens (JCGB). Monument to family on wall (*LN*, Vol. 4, p. 140). Either MP or his father on Congregational Union committee, 1879 (*CYB*, 1879, p. 17).

ODNB (mentioning that father and brothers Congregationalists). *WWBMP* 2.

SAMUEL PLIMSOLL
10 Feb. 1824 - 3 June 1898
MP (L) for Derby, 1868 - Apr. 1880

Coal merchant. Secretary of Sheffield Great Exhibition committee, 1851. Promoted Merchant Shipping Act, 1876, requiring "Plimsoll mark". Defeated candidate at Derby, 1865; Liverpool, 1880; and Sheffield, Central, 1885. Supported arbitration for workers' rights and special care for orphans outside workhouse (1880). President of Sailors' and Fireman's Union, 1890. Published *Our Seamen: An Appeal* (1873). Of 28 Park Lane, London.

Member of Nether Church, Sheffield, where suspended for bankruptcy in 1855 and subsequently restored. In later life associated with Tontine Street Congregational Church, Folkestone, where he lived from 1892. (Surman) Brother-in-law of F. J. Falding, principal of Rotherham College (JCGB).

David Masters, *The Plimsoll Mark* (London, 1955). *ODNB. BDMBR* 3 (omitting religion). *WWBMP.*

Sir CHARLES REED
20 June 1819 - 25 Mar. 1881
MP (L) for Hackney, 1868 - Apr. 1874 (unseated on petition)
St Ives, Cornwall, 1880-81

Printer, co-founder of Tyler and Reed (1842), then (1849-61) in partnership with Benjamin Patton and finally founder of Sir Charles Reed and Sons, typefounders. Son of Andrew Reed, Congregational minister of Hackney. Madras House, Hackney; Hackney Grammar School; Silcoates School; University College, London. Married Margaret, daughter of Edward Baines, sen. Secretary of Leeds Literary Institution. Co-editor of *Leeds Repository* from 1839, supporting Anti-Corn Law League. Promoted Sunday School Union at Leeds. Secretary of London committee opposing Graham's education clauses in factory bill, 1843. On committee of London Sunday School Union from 1844, visiting Sunday schools round the country as its deputation and winning its first prize for *The Infant Class in the Sunday School* (1851). Published addresses on education of poor including *Diamonds in the Dust* (1866) and *The Teacher's Keys* (1872). Common Councillor, City of London, from 1855, carrying resolution in favour of abolition of university tests in 1866. Commissioner of lieutenancy for London, 1862. Published *The Nonconformist Elector* weekly during 1847 election. Member (from 1847), vice-chairman (1863-67) and chairman (1867-74) of Dissenting Deputies (Manning, p. 486). Vice-chairman (1870-73) and chairman (1873-81) of London School

Board, defending Bible teaching. On committee of City of London School. Opposed Sunday labour in Post Office. In maiden speech in Commons secured exemption of Sunday schools and Ragged Schools from poor rates. Opposed to all religious endowments in Ireland and favoured redistribution of seats (1881). Voted against Bradlaugh. Knight, 1874. LLD, Yale, 1873. Author of *Why not? A Plea for a Free Public Library and Museum in the City of London* (1855) and co-edited *Memoirs of the Life and Philanthropic Labours of Andrew Reed, D.D.* (1863). Director and Trustee of Abney Park Cemetery from 1866. Chairman of Bunhill Fields Preservation Society from 1865. Antiquary, collecting MSS and keys. FSA. Author (with Joseph Beck) of *An Historical Narrative of . . . the Honourable the Irish Society* (1865). Of Earlsmead, Page Green, Tottenham. According to James Guinness Rogers, a Silcoates classmate, Reed was "amiable, gentle, considerate, and kind" (*Congregationalist*, May 1881, p.367).

Converted on visit of David Abeel, American missionary, to Silcoates. Joined his father's Wycliffe Chapel, Whitechapel, 1835. Attended Salem Chapel, Leeds (1838-44), where taught in Sunday school. Secretary of Leeds Sunday School Union, 1839. Considered entering ministry. After return to Hackney, 1844, remained member of his father's church, but usually attended Old Gravel Pit under Pye Smith and then John Davies. When this church moved to Clapton Park, he migrated with it, becoming deacon. On committee of Religious Tract Society, supporting start of *Boys' Own*. On committee of British and Foreign Bible Society for nearly 20 years and of LMS. Supported founding of Homerton College by Congregational Board of Education. Addressed Congregational Union assembly on Sunday schools, 1853, 1859 and 1860.

C. E. B. Reed, *Memoir of Sir Charles Reed* (London, 1883). *ODNB. BDEB.* Boase. *Congregationalist*, May 1881, pp. 361-7.

HENRY RICHARD
3 Apr. 1812 - 20 Aug. 1888
MP (L) for Merthyr Tydfil, 1868-88

Minister. Son of Ebenezer Richard, Calvinistic Methodist minister. Llangeitho Grammar School; and Highbury College, 1830-34. Minister of Marlborough Chapel, Old Kent Road, London, 1835-50. Secretary of Peace Society, 1848-85, organising peace congresses, 1849-53, and editing *Herald of Peace*. Held dinner party on day of public fasting for Crimean War in 1854 (Miall, p. 103). Helped secure arbitration clause in treaty of Paris, 1856. Carried Commons motion in favour of international arbitration, 8 July 1873. Secretary of Voluntary School Association from 1847. Chairman of Dissenting Deputies, 1875-88. Member of executive committee of Liberation Society from 1851, and of central committee from 1865. Travelled in Wales as Liberation Society deputation, 1862, rousing latent Liberalism. Seconded Edward Miall's motion for English disestablishment, 9 May 1871. Champion of Wales against "Treachery of the Blue Books", 1847, and in Commons. Associated with University College of Wales, Aberystwyth. The only Nonconformist on Aberdare Committee to investigate intermediate and higher education in Wales, 1880. Presided at National Eisteddfod, Merthyr, 1881. Member of Royal Commission on Education, 1886-88, recommending use of Welsh in elementary schools. Author of *Defensive War* (1846), *History of the War against Russia* (1855), *Memoirs of Joseph Sturge* (1866), *Letters on the Social and Political Condition of the Principality of Wales* (1866), *The Recent Progress of International Arbitration* (1884), and (with Carvell Williams) *Disestablishment* (1885). "[T]he parliamentary leader of the Nonconformists" (*Congregationalist*, Apr. 1882, p. 266).

Attended Kensington Chapel from early 1860s, becoming attached to Alexander Raleigh, minister from 1875 to 1880 (Miall, pp. 370, 378). Helped form society for supporting English Congregational chapels in S Wales, 1860. Chairman of Congregational Union, 1877, when seen as layman (Miall, p. 281).

C. S. Miall, *Henry Richard, M. P.* (London, 1889). *ODNB. BDMBR* 3. Boase. *Congregationalist* , Apr. 1882, pp. 265-9. *T* , 22 Aug. 1888 (and after). Papers at National Library of Wales.

EVAN MATTHEW RICHARDS

1821 - 21 Aug. 1880

MP (L) for Cardiganshire, 1868-74

Steel manufacturer; partner of L. L. Dillwyn, MP, in Landore Steel Works. Previously partner in Birmingham hardware firm and manager of Onllwyn Iron works, which failed. Member of Swansea town council from 1853; mayor, 1855 and 1862-63. Favoured county finance boards to reduce rates and had confidence in "the wisdom and integrity of Mr. Gladstone" (1873). Contested Honiton, 1865; and Cardiganshire, 1874. JP, DL. Of Brooklands, near Swansea.

Funeral at Bethel Welsh Independent Chapel, Sketty, Swansea, conducted by Independent ministers (*The Cambrian* obituary). Often described as Baptist because his wife was member of Mount Pleasant English Baptist Chapel, Swansea, and he attended with her (T. M. Bassett, *The Welsh Baptists* (Swansea, 1977), p. 302).

WWBMP. Boase. I. G. Jones, "Cardiganshire Politics in the Mid-Nineteenth Century", *Ceredigion* 5 (1964), pp. 32-5.

Sir HENRY WILLIAM RIPLEY
23 Apr. 1813 - 9 Nov. 1882
MP (L) for Bradford, 1868 - Mar. 1869 (unseated on petition)
(LC) for Bradford, 1874-80
Dyer of Bradford; senior partner of Edward Ripley and Son. Began managing father's firm in 1833, building it up to dominate Bowling. His technique of rainbow dyeing, treating animal and vegetable fibres together, enabled mixed-worsted fabrics to flourish in Bradford (Koditschek, pp. 175, 231). Chairman of Bradford Old Bank. Horton House School, Bradford. Married Susan, daughter of Robert Milligan, MP. Turned from Liberal into "A Moderate Conservative" (1880). Defeated Edward Miall at 1868 election. Himself defeated by Alfred Illingworth at Bradford, 1880. Bradford councillor, 1850-53, and alderman, 1859-60. First president of Philosophical Society. Vice-president of Mechanics' Institution, heading list of subscribers to building fund with £1,200. A founder of Bradford Chamber of Commerce, 1852; president, 1858-68; chairman of its postal committee, promoting postal communication at home and abroad; first president of executive of Association of Chambers of Commerce, 1859. Advised Cobden over commercial treaty with France, 1860. Host to Palmerston on his visit to lay foundation stone of Bradford Wool Exchange, 9 Aug. 1864. Member of co-operative trading societies commission. Built Ripleyville suburb of model houses for his workers from 1865. Regretting loss of "a certain sociability and freedom of intercourse which had since passed away", he wanted to make "those with whom he came in contact feel that he was not merely their master but one of themselves, as far as it was possible for a master to be" (*Bradford Observer*, 20 Oct. 1868, quoted by Koditschek, pp. 432-3). Provided school at Ripleyville and supported Borough West School. Supported technical education late in life. Built Woodlands Convalescent Home, 1877, costing over £20,000. JP, DL. Bart, 1880. Died at Bedstone Court, Salop, but previously of Acacia, Apperley, Leeds.

Member of Horton Lane Congregational Chapel, Bradford, joining 1840 (JCGB). Laid foundation stone of new Horton Lane Chapel, Sept. 1861, and defrayed 10% of cost of building (*Bradford Observer*, 11 Nov. 1882, p. 7). Said to be practising Anglican by the late 1860s (T. Jowitt, "The Pattern of Religion in Victorian Bradford", in D. G. Wright and J. A. Jowitt (eds), *Victorian Bradford* (Bradford, 1982), p. 48). Gave land for St Bartholomew's Church, Ripleyville, 1871, still denying he was Churchman. But vice-president of Bradford Church Institute, 1876-79. (*Bradford Observer*, 11 Nov. 1882, p. 7).

WWBMP. Boase. Theodore Koditschek, *Class Formation and Urban-Industrial Society: Bradford, 1750-1850* (Cambridge, 1990). *Bradford Observer*, 11 Nov. 1882, p. 7.

JOSEPH RUSTON

Feb. 1835 - 10 June 1897

MP (L) for Lincoln, June 1884-86

Manufacturer of engineering products. Educated at Wesley College, Sheffield. Apprenticed to Sheffield cutlery firm. Formed Ruston, Proctor and Co. at Lincoln, 1857, making agricultural implements but branching out into variety of steam engines, boilers and pumps. Using motto "My customer is my best friend", he gained a global market. Supplied 70 excavators for Manchester Ship Canal. At death his firm had over 2,500 employees and a branch in Budapest. Chairman of Joseph Rogers and Sons Ltd, Sheffield cutlers, and Lincolnshire Publishing Co. Ltd. Member of Lincoln city council, 1865; alderman, 1874; mayor, 1869-70. High Sheriff of Lincs, 1891. First freeman of Lincoln, 1891. Although "a warm supporter of Mr.Gladstone's Government" (1886), he voted against Home Rule and declined to stand in 1886. Paid for Drill Hall for Lincoln Volunteers, 1890. President of Lincoln committee of NSPCC. Paid for children's ward at city hospital, 1892. Chairman of Lincolnshire Agricultural Society, 1892. JP, DL. Chevalier of Legion of Honour. Art collector. Underwrote restoration of Queen Eleanor's tomb in cathedral. Of Monk's Manor, near Lincoln.

Member of Newland Congregational Church, Lincoln; deacon from 1865. Treasurer of Lincolnshire Congregational Union and chairman, 1887-88 (JCGB). Largely responsible for new building of his church. "He is ... the most prominent and active Congregational layman in the county." (*Congregationalist,* Oct. 1884, p. 801). Supported mission halls at South Bar and Croft Street, Lincoln. President of Lincoln YMCA. On committee of Congregational Union, 1879 and 1887 (*CYB*, 1879, p. 17; 1887, p. xix). Gave J. D. Jones a sense of the difficulties of a Christian businessman in wanting to do his duty by his employees and fellow employers. (J. D. Jones, *Three Score Years and Ten* (London, 1940), p. 43).

ODNB. WWBMP. T, 12 June 1897, p. 10. www.oldengine.org/members/ruston/History1.htm. Commonplace book in Lincolnshire Archives.

ENOCH ROBERT GIBBON SALISBURY

7 Nov. 1819 - 27 Oct. 1890

MP (L) for Chester, 1857-59

Proprietor of gas works. Called to bar, Inner Temple, 1852, practising at Parliamentary Bar. Considered birth-right, servitude, education and taxation to be qualifications for franchise; favoured ballot and more equal distribution of ecclesiastical revenues (1858). Defeated candidate at Chester, 1859 and 1868. Wrote *A Letter on National Education* (1849), and

Border Counties Worthies (1880). Bibliophile, assembling library on Wales now at University College, Cardiff. Of 5 Stanley Place, Chester, and later Glen-aber, Saltney, near Chester.

Congregationalist. Married Sarah, daughter of Arthur Jones, DD, Independent minister of Bangor. Also brother-in-law of Congregational minister (JCGB). Presumably member of Northgate Street Congregational Chapel, Chester.

ODNB (omitting religion). *DWB. WWBMP.* Boase.

Sir TITUS SALT
20 Sept. 1803 - 29 Dec. 1876
MP (L) for Bradford, 1859 - Jan. 1861

Textile manufacturer, concentrating on alpaca. Batley Grammar School and Heath Grammar School, Wakefield. President of Bradford Chamber of Commerce, 1856. Chief constable of Bradford; second mayor, 1848-49. A founder of *Bradford Observer*, 1833; of Bradford Reform Association, 1835; and of United Reform Society, 1841. In 1842, chaired anti-Corn Law meeting which endorsed six points of Charter. Treasurer of Congregational electoral committee at Bradford, 1847 (A. Jowitt, "Dissenters, Voluntaryism and Liberal Unity: The 1847 Election", in J. A. Jowitt and R. K. S. Taylor (eds), *Nineteenth-Century Bradford Elections* (Bradford, 1879), p. 15). Chairman of Bradford Registration Reform Society in 1850s (Jack Reynolds, "The General Election of 1859, Bradford", in *ibid.*, p. 40). Supported Reform League and Reform Union, 1867. Favoured parliamentary reform, ballot and non-intervention in continental politics, though army and navy to be efficient for self-defence (1860), but "within the walls of St Stephen's his voice was never heard, except on some formal occasion, such as the presentation of a petition" (Balgarnie, p. 189). Supported Liberation Society, once giving £5,000 (Balgarnie, p. 268). JP, DL. Bart, 1869. Colonel of Volunteers. On board of Bradford Mechanics' Institute, 1850. President of Bradford Freehold Land Building Society, 1849. Gave railway excursion to employees, 1849, but tolerated no unions. Creator of Saltaire model village from 1853, equipped with school, institute, almshouses, Congregational and Methodist chapels, bath and wash houses and park. Gave more than £250,000 to charities, 1846-76. Spoke with pronounced Yorkshire accent (Reynolds, p. 37). Of Crowe Nest, Lightcliffe, from 1844 and of Methley Park from 1858.

Baptised at Old New Independent Chapel, Morley, 1803 (and also at Batley Parish Church, 1805). Family attended Horton Lane Independent Chapel, Bradford, where Titus became Sunday school librarian, teacher and superintendent. Father, though never a church member, was on the building committee of Salem Chapel, Bradford. Titus' wife Caroline joined Horton Lane in 1838-39, transferring to Bramley Lane, Lightcliffe, Congregational Chapel in 1845 (*BDMBR* 2). Titus erected Saltaire Congregational Chapel, 1858. Did not make public profession of faith until he first took communion at Saltaire in 1861 (so that technically Salt was not a Congregational MP). Attended parish church at Methley in 1860s, perhaps, like two of his sons, contemplating adhesion to C. of E. (Reynolds, p. 83). Chairman of building committee of Lightcliffe, 1871, where he attended. In London worshipped at Westminster Chapel, where Samuel Martin held weekly devotional meeting for MPs. Founded Bradford Town Mission, 1851, supporting Bible women especially. (Balgarnie, pp. 13, 40, 75-6, 197-8, 260, 265) Gave £2,500 for Airedale Independent College, whose foundation stone he laid, 1874, thereby retaining it at Bradford (K. W. Wadsworth, *Yorkshire United Independent College* (London, 1954), p. 124), and £5,000 for Memorial Hall (Peel, p. 277). His son Titus sat on Congregational Union committee from 1871 (*CYB*, 1871, p. ix).

Robert Balgarnie, *Sir Titus Salt, Baronet* (London, 1877). Jack Reynolds, *The Great Paternalist: Titus Salt and the Growth of Nineteenth-Century Bradford* (London,1983). *ODNB. BDMBR* 2 (JCGB). *WWBMP.* Boase. D. H. Mason, *Ten Thousand Sermons, 1871-1971: The People, Parsons and Praise of Lightcliffe Congregational Church* (Lightcliffe, 1971).

Sir THEODORE FREDERICK CHARLES EDWARD SHAW
11 Sept. 1859 - 17 Apr. 1942
MP (L) for Stafford, 1892 - Dec. 1910

Merchant; chairman of John Shaw and Sons, Wolverhampton. Tettenhall College; Balliol College, Oxford. Twice member of Wolverhampton town council. Favoured registration reform, disestablishment, land law reform, popular control of liquor traffic, one man one vote, all elections on one day (1910). Passive resister. Captain of 3rd Volunteer Battalion, S Staffs Regiment. Bart, 1908. Wrote numerous newspaper articles, chiefly from abroad. Of Tettenhall, Wolverhampton (1906). At death, of Harewood, Sunninghill, Berks.

Free Churchman (*FCYB*, 1907, p. 260). Son of Edward Dethick Shaw, member and Sunday school teacher of Queen Street Congregational Church, Wolverhampton (H. A. May, *Queen Street Congregational Church, Wolverhampton* ([Wolverhampton], 1909), p. 37). MP likely also to have been member.

WWW 1941-1950. *WWBMP* 2.

THOMAS SHAW
    21 Dec. 1823 - 15 Jan. 1893
    MP (L) for Halifax, Aug. 1882 - Jan. 1893

    Woollen manufacturer and merchant; chairman of John Shaw and Sons Ltd,
    Brookroyd Mill, near Halifax. Huddersfield College. Hon. treasurer of
    Anti-Corn Law League. Member of Halifax town council from 1865;
    mayor, 1866-68. President of Halifax Chamber of Commerce, 1874-76.
    President of Halifax Mechanics' Institute for many years from 1872.
    Favoured "Mr. Gladstone's policy, specially in Ireland" (1892). JP, DL. Of
    Allangate, Halifax, and Oakes House, Stainland, Yorks.

    Member of Holywell Green Congregational Church (JCGB).

    WWBMP. Boase. *CW*, 19 Jan. 1893, p. 42. *T*, 16 Jan. 1893, p. 10.

WILLIAM SHAW
    4 May 1823 - 19 Sept. 1895
    MP (L) for Bandon, 1868-74
    MP (Home Rule) for County Cork, 1874-85

    Son of Samuel Shaw, Independent minister. Tettenhall College (JCGB);
    Trinity College, Dublin, without degree; Highbury College. Minister of
    George's Street Independent Church, Cork, 1846-50. Married into wealthy
    Cork merchant family, 1850, and became director of several Cork
    businesses. Chairman of Munster Bank, which collapsed in 1885. Bank-
    rupt, Jan. 1886. Connected with Young Ireland as young man. Unsuccessful
    candidate at Bandon twice in 1865. Presided at Dublin conference to found
    Home Rule League, 1873. Elected chairman of Irish Home Rule Party after
    death of Isaac Butt, May 1879. Held aloof from Irish National Land
    League, defeated as chairman by C. S. Parnell, May 1880, and led
    secession of pro-Liberal Home Rulers, Jan. 1881. (C. C. O'Brien, *Parnell
    and his Party* (Oxford, 1957), pp. 5, 24n., 25, 46, 56). Resigned from Home
    Rule League, Dec. 1881. Retired from politics, 1885. Member of
    Bessborough Commission, 1880. "Sensible Shaw". Of Beaumont, Cork.

    ODNB. Boase. *T*, 24 Sept. 1895, p. 7.

ALBERT SPICER
    16 Mar. 1847 - 20 Dec. 1934
    MP (L) for Monmouth District, 1892-1900
    Hackney Central, 1906-18

    Paper maker; director of James Spicer and Sons. Mill Hill School;
    Heidelberg, learning German. Regretted lack of university education
    (Spicer, p. 24). Studied J. S. Mill and Henry George, deciding in favour of

tax on capital value of land (p. 36). Member of Fishmongers' Company. President of London Chamber of Commerce, 1907-10. President of Congress of Chambers of Commerce of the Empire, Sydney, 1909. Member of Commercial Intelligence Advisory Committee, Board of Trade, 1907-17. Member of Advisory Committee to Army Council on the Spiritual and Moral Welfare of the Army, 1907-14. Joint treasurer, and vice-chairman, 1907-17, State Children's Association, placing Poor Law orphans in good homes. Chairman of Marconi Committee, 1912. Member of Royal Commission on Paper, 1916-18. Member of Woodford School Board, 1877-93. Vice-president of London and Home Counties Liberal Union. Trustee of National Liberal Club. Unsuccessful candidate for Walthamstow, 1886; and for Monmouth District, 1900 and May 1901. "He was not an orator, and his speeches were rare though always straight and to the point and absolutely honest." (Spicer, p. 38). Free trader, but favoured strengthening ties with empire (pp. 40-1). Bart, 1906. PC, 1912. JP. Passive resister. Gave away 26% of income during active life (Spicer, p. 18): "a Victorian of the best type" (J. D. Jones, quoted Spicer, p. 8). Of 10 Lancaster Gate, London.

Son of James Spicer, treasurer of Congregational Union, 1874-88 (Albert Peel, *The Congregational Two Hundred, 1530-1948* (London, 1948), p. 240). Member, deacon and Sunday school superintendent at Woodford Congregational Church. On executive of Essex Congregational Union. Treasurer and chairman of London Congregational Union. (*Congregationalist*, Feb. 1883, pp. 98-9). Trustee of Christ Church, Westminster Bridge Road . Seatholder of Paddington Chapel to 1909. (JCGB) Active at King's Weigh House until 1909 (Elaine Kaye, *The History of the King's Weigh House Church* (London, 1968), p. 114). In his latter years his favourite preachers were G. Campbell Morgan and J. H. Jowett of Westminster Chapel (Spicer, p. 25), where he was deacon (Peel, *Congregational Two Hundred*, p. 241). Director of LMS from 1873; chairman of board, 1882; treasurer, 1885-1910. Treasurer (1885-1921), trustee and member of council, Mansfield College, Oxford. Chairman of Congregational Union, 1893 (first layman, not counting Henry Richard). Chairman of Twentieth Century Fund from 1899. Chairman of council of Congregational Union, 1907. Moderator of International Congregational Council, Boston, 1899. Chairman of C. U. Laymen's Commission from 1919. President, Mill Hill School. President of Sunday School Union, 1900. Vice-president of British and Foreign Bible Society, 1896. "The truths which inspired my father were those of evangelical Christianity, though he never liked the adjective.... He was not much interested in doctrinal matters – he was content to leave that to the experts." (Spicer, pp. 9, 21-2).

[S. D. Spicer], *Albert Spicer, 1847-1934: A Man of his Time by One of his Family* (London, 1938). *ODNB. WWW* 1929-40. *WWBMP* 2. *Congregationalist*, Feb. 1883, pp. 97-100.

HENRY SPICER
1837 - 18 Oct. 1915
MP (L) for Islington, S, 1885-86

Wholesale stationer; member of Spicer Brothers. Son of Henry Spicer; cousin of Albert Spicer. Mill Hill School; New College, St John's Wood, graduating from London University. Member of Fishmongers' Company. Member of London School Board from 1879, chairing Industrial Schools committee. Defeated at Islington, S, 1886. JP. Fellow of the Geographical and Zoological Societies. Of 14 Aberdeen Park, Highbury.

Deacon of Union Chapel, Islington. Married daughter of Dr Joseph Mullens, Foreign Secretary of LMS. (JCGB).

WWBMP.

Sir HALLEY STEWART
18 Jan. 1838 - 26 Jan. 1937
MP (L) for Lincolnshire, Spalding, July 1887-95
Greenock, 1906 - Jan. 1910

Vice-chairman, London Brick Co. Partner in Stewart Brothers and Spencer, cattle cake manufacturers in Rochester, 1870-95. Editor of *Hastings and St Leonards Times,* 1877-83. JP. Knight, 1932. Fellow of King's College, London, 1936. President of Liberation Society. President of Secular Education League. Favoured adult suffrage for both sexes, religious equality, land for the people, abolition of House of Lords (1909). Defeated in Spalding, 1885, 1886 and 1895; and in Peterborough, 1900. Founder of Sir Halley Stewart Trust, 1924. Moved from St Leonard's to Clapham Park, 1894. Latterly of The Red House, Harpenden, Herts.

Son of Alexander Stewart, Independent minister, Barnet. Brother was George Stewart, Congregational minister (*CW*, 3 Jan. 1907, p. 3). Pastor of Croft Chapel, Hastings, 1863-74, and Caledonian Road Church, London, 1874-77, though not ordained. Treasurer of Sussex County Congregational Association for 15 years to 1894. Member of Harpenden Congregational Church, promoting minimum stipend for Hertfordshire ministers (1919-20), supporting Luton Road Mission and preaching in every Congregational church in the county (Newton, pp. 33, 76,114-15, 173). Member of Congregational Union committee (*CYB*, 1886, p. xix).

David Newton, *Sir Halley Stewart* (London, 1968). *ODNB. WWW* 1929-1940. *WWBMP* 2.

THEODORE COOKE TAYLOR

3 Aug. 1850 - 19 Oct. 1952

MP (L) for Lancashire, SE, Radcliffe-cum-Farnworth, 1900-18

Woollen manufacturer; head of J., T., and J. Taylor Ltd. Batley Grammar School and Silcoates School. Member of West Riding CC, 1889-92. JP. Active in anti-opium movement, visiting China in 1907. Maiden speech in Commons for old age pensions. Commenced profit-sharing scheme, 1892, distributing over £2,240,000 to his employees, and became tireless advocate of the principle. Supported Batley Co-operative Society. Made benefactions to town mission, district hospital, maternity home. Lifelong member of Batley Temperance Society. Non-smoker. Began public speaking during Bulgarian horrors. (Greenwood, p. 9). Passive resister. Of Sunny Bank, Batley.

Deacon of Batley Congregational Church for over 65 years. Sunday school teacher and superintendent, 1886-91. Leader of Pleasant Sunday Afternoon, 1891-1922. Left legacy to Congregational Union (Greenwood, p. 158).

G. A. Greenwood, *Taylor of Batley* (London, 1957). T. C. Taylor, *One Hundred Years: Records, Recollections and Reflections* (Leeds, 1946). Sidney Pollard and R. Turner, "Profit Sharing and Autocracy: The Case of J. T. and J. Taylor of Batley, Woollen Manufacturers, 1892-1966", *Business History* 18 (1976), 4-34. *ODNB* (mentioning that he was Congregationalist, but stating that he supported financially "the local Congregational Union"). *WWW* 1951-1960. *WWBMP* 2.

Sir FREDERICK WHITLEY THOMSON

2 Sept. 1851 - 21 June 1925

MP (L) for Yorkshire, West Riding, N, Skipton, 1900-05

Director of English Card Clothing Co. Ltd. Mother was Emma Whitley. Educated Glasgow Academy and Andersonian Institution, Glasgow. President of Halifax Chamber of Commerce, 1912-14. Alderman (1908) and mayor of Halifax (1908-11). Contested S Herefordshire, Jan. 1908; Colchester, Jan.1910. JP. Knight, 1916. Médaille du Roi (Belgium) for services to Belgian refugees during First World War. Changed name to Whitley-Thomson, 1914. Of Savile Heath, Halifax.

Deacon of Park Church, Halifax (*CW*, 19 Oct. 1909, p. 3).

WWW 1916-1928. *WWBMP* 2.

JACOB HENRY TILLETT

1 Nov. 1818 - 30 Jan. 1892

MP (L) for Norwich, July 1870 - Jan. 1871 (unseated on petition), Mar.-May 1875 (unseated on petition), 1880-85

Solicitor at Norwich, 1839-72. Editor and proprietor of *Norfolk News,* 1845-92. Norwich Grammar School. Alderman of Norwich; mayor, 1859 and 1875. Member of Norwich School Board, 1871-80; chairman, 1877-80. Contested Norwich, 1868, 1874 and 1886. Favoured extension of county franchise and reform of land laws (1885). Of Carrow Abbey, Norwich.

Brought up at Tabernacle and became member of Prince's Street Congregational Church, Norwich (Information from C. B. Jewson). Addressed Congregational Union meeting for working men on "Protestantism" at Ipswich, 15 Oct. 1873 (*CYB,* 1874, p. 84). Spoke at laying of memorial stone of Cowper Congregational Church, East Dereham, Norfolk (*Evangelical Magazine,* Oct. 1873, p. 604).

WWBMP. Boase.

ROBERT WALLACE
1850 - 19 Mar. 1939
MP (L) for Perth, 1895-1907

Barrister. Wesley College; Queen's University, Belfast. Called to bar, Middle Temple, 1874. Served on NE Circuit. Examiner of Court and Revising Barrister for Middlesex. Chairman of County of London Sessions, 1907-31. Contested Wandsworth, 1885; Edinburgh, W, 1886; Renfrewshire, W, 1892. QC, 1894. Knight, 1916. Of 32 Clarence Gate Gardens, London.

Son of Robert Wallace, Dublin Presbyterian minister. Thought to be Scottish Presbyterian (*CW,* 27 Dec. 1906, p. 3), but regular hearer of C. S. Horne at Kensington and treasurer of Whitefield's Tabernacle from 1903 (W. B. Selbie, *The Life of Charles Silvester Horne, M.A., M. P.* (London, 1920), pp. 176, 263).

WWW 1929-1940. *WWBMP* 2.

Sir CORNELIUS MARSHALL WARMINGTON
1842 - 12 Dec. 1908
MP (L) for Monmouthshire, W, 1885-95

Barrister. University College, London. Called to bar, Middle Temple, 1869; bencher, 1885. QC, 1882. Bart, 1908. Of 43 Courtfield Gardens, London.

Member of Lion Walk Congregational Church, Colchester, 1862-67. Transferred to Kentish Town Congregational Church. (JCGB).

WW 1897-1916. *WWBMP* 2.

THOMAS WAYMAN
26 Oct. 1833 - 8 Feb. 1901
MP (L) for Yorkshire, West Riding, N, Elland, 1885-99

Wool merchant, retiring 1892. Son of W. H. Wayman, cardmaker. Mayor of Halifax, 1872-74. Favoured maintaining constitution, but reforming Lords (1898). Governor of Crossley Orphanage. Of Oaklands, Clapham Park, London; retired to Banbury.

Member of Park Chapel, Halifax, unsuccessfully inviting J. A. Macfadyen to its pulpit, 1869 (Alexander Mackennal, *Life of John Allison Macfadyen, M.A., D.D.* (London, 1891), p. 217).

WWW 1897-1916. *WWBMP* 2.

Sir JOSEPH DODGE WESTON
1822 - 5 Mar. 1895
MP (L) for Bristol, S, 1885-86
Bristol, E, May 1890 - Mar. 1895

Proprietor of Bristol Wagon and Carriage Works. Bishop's College, Clifton. Originally partner with father Thomas in iron and hardware business, Redcliffe Square, Bristol. Joined brother in shipping trade. Partner in ironworks at Cwm, near Newport, Mon., amalgamating with Patent Nut and Bolt Co., of which chairman many years. Chairman of Great Western Cotton Co., 1885. Member of Bristol town council from 1868; mayor, 1880-84. Brought about resolution of debate about site of docks by purchasing Avonmouth for the town, 1884, though had previously supported its rival Portishead while Samuel Morley endorsed Avonmouth and W. H. Wills backed Bristol itself (Latimer, pp. 399-400). Chairman of Bristol Liberal Federation. Favoured promoting industrial exhibitions. Supported Bristol Infirmary and new children's hospital. Led campaign for free public libraries. Succeeded Samuel Morley as MP at Bristol and Handel Cossham at Bristol, E. Defeated at Bristol, S, 1886. Knight, 1886. JP. Of Dorset House, Clifton Down, Bristol.

Congregationalist (*Christian Life*, 20 Aug. 1892, p. 399). Baptised at Castle Green Independent Chapel, Bristol (http://archiver.rootsweb.com/th/read/Bristol_and_Somerset/1998-02/0886861312), where may well have become member.

WWBMP 2. Boase. H. E. Meller, *Leisure and the Changing City, 1870-1914* (London, 1976), p. 89 (though failing to identify religion beyond "Nonconformist"). *T*, 6 Mar. 1895, p. 10. John Latimer, *The Annals of Bristol in the Nineteenth Century* (Bristol, 1887).

JOHN HENRY WHITLEY

8 Feb. 1866 - 3 Feb. 1935

MP (L) for Halifax, 1900-28

Cotton spinner. Clifton College; London University. Member of Halifax town council, 1893-1900. Junior Lord of Treasury, 1907-10. Deputy Chairman of Ways and Means, 1910. Chairman of Ways and Means and Deputy Speaker, 1911-21. Chairman of Committee on the Relations of Employers and Employed, 1916-18, establishing Whitley Councils. Speaker of the Commons, 1921-28. Chairman of Royal Commission on Labour in India, 1929-31. Chairman of BBC, 1930-35. President of Clifton College. President of National Council of Social Service from 1921. PC, 1911. DCL (Oxon), LLD (Cantab and Leeds). Kaiser-i-Hind Medal (First Class), 1932. JP. Of Brantwood, Halifax.

Member of Park Church, Halifax; and Sunday school teacher (Surman). One son, Percy, was deacon of Park Church; another, Oliver, was deacon at Church of Peace of God, Oxted, Surrey (JCGB).

ODNB (not mentioning religion). *WWW* 1929-1940. *WWBMP* 3.

BENJAMIN WHITWORTH

1816 - 24 Sept. 1893

MP (L) for Drogheda, 1865 - Jan. 1869 (unseated on petition), Mar. 1880-85

Kilkenny, Apr. 1875 - Feb. 1880

Cotton manufacturer and merchant; partner in B. Whitworth and Brothers, 1838-93. Introduced manufacture of cotton to Drogheda, *c.* 1863. Director of Metropolitan Railway. Lived at Fleetwood, 1849-62. Contested Stafford, June 1869; Drogheda, 1874; and Lewisham, 1885. Member of executive of United Kingdom Alliance from 1863 and chairman, 1871-91. Vice-president of British Temperance League. Threatened in 1883 to disobey the Liberal whip in order to force government to attend to temperance demands. LU after Home Rule split, putting the issue before temperance (A. E. Dingle, *The Campaign for Prohibition in Victorian England* (London, 1980), pp. 93,100). Supported Liberation Society, women's enfranchisement, Sunday opening of museums. Built institutes at Fleetwood (1863) and Drogheda (1864-65). Of 22 Daleham Gardens, Hampstead.

Member of Fleetwood Congregational Church? Gave money for school at Wesham and for supporting evangelist in the Fylde (*LN*, Vol. 1, pp. 102, 134, 200). At end of life attended Lyndhurst Road Congregational Church, Hampstead (Binfield, p. 134n).

J. C. G. Binfield, "The Shaping of a Dissenting Interest", in Stephen Taylor and David L. Wykes (eds), *Parliament and Dissent* (Edinburgh, 2005), pp. 120-35. *WWBMP.* Boase. Brian Harrrison, *Dictionary of British Temperance Biography* (Coventry, 1973), p. 136. *T,* 26 Sept. 1893, p. 7.

JOHN WILKS
1776 - 25 Aug. 1854
MP (L) for Boston, July 1830-37

Attorney, retiring 1825. Founder and hon. secretary of Protestant Society for the Protection of Religious Liberty, 1811. Contested Boston, 1826, and St Albans, 1847. "The politics of Mr. Wilks were always extremely Radical, and particularly on those points in which the Dissenters took an interest" (*Gentleman's Magazine*, Dec. 1854, p. 629). JP. Fellow of the Royal Statistical and Zoological Societies. Member of the London Institution. Trustee of the Westminster Club. Member of the Whig Club. Bibliophile and art collector. Collection sold after death by Sotheby and Wilkinson. Of 3 Finsbury Square, London.

Son of Matthew Wilks, minister of Whitefield's Tabernacle. Acted for Hoxton Academy. Contributed to Congregational Library. Supported LMS, writing *An Apology for the Missionary Society* (1799). Daughter married James Parsons, Congregational minister at York.

ODNB (omitting subject's religion). *BDEB. WWBMP*. Boase. *Gentleman's Magazine,* Dec. 1854, p. 629. Papers of Protestant Society at Dr Williams's Library.

JOHN CARVELL WILLIAMS
20 Sept. 1821 - 8 Oct. 1907
MP (L) for Nottingham, S, 1885-86
Nottinghamshire, Mansfield, 1892-1900

Ecclesiastical lawyer in Doctors' Commons. Secretary of local committee opposing education clauses of Graham's factory bill, 1843, which turned into E London Religious Liberty Society. Member of Liberation Society executive from its inception, 1844; secretary from 1847, then vice-president; chairman of its parliamentary committee from 1865; and chairman of society from 1877. Editor of *The Liberator* from 1855. Subsidised society in 1890s (D. W. Bebbington, *The Nonconformist Conscience* (London, 1982), p. 20). Retired from office in Liberation Society, 1906. Member of Dissenting Deputies. Most concerned with religious inequalities in burial laws. Carried bill for extending hours for solemnising marriage, 1886. Co-author with Henry Richard of

Disestablishment (1885). President of Hornsey Liberal Association by 1889. "An advanced liberal, in favour of Home Rule, disestablishment, unsectarian education, temperance legislation and international arbitration" (1900). Defeated at Nottingham, S, 1886. Of Hornsey Rise Gardens, London.

Brought up at Stepney Meeting. Member of Claremont Congregational Chapel, Pentonville. Deacon of Surbiton Congregational Chapel. Member of Park Chapel, Crouch End, from 1872. Supported building of Stroud Green Congregational Church, Essex. Member of Congregational Union committee (*CYB*, 1886, p. xviii). Chairman of Congregational Union, 1899 (*CW*, 10 Oct. 1907, p. 11).

H. Welch, "John Carvell Williams, the Nonconformist Watchdog (1821-1907)" (Kansas PhD, 1968). *ODNB. BDMBR* 3. *WWW* 1897-1916. *WWBMP* 2.

WILLIAM WILLIAMS
1840 - 21 Apr. 1904
MP (L) for Swansea District, June 1893-95

Tin-plate manufacturer; proprietor of Forest Steel and Tin-Plate works, Morriston, where had worked as a boy. Also owned Worcester and Morlais Tin-Plate Works, Morriston. Deputy chairman of Glamorganshire Banking Co. Member of Swansea town council, 1879-88; mayor. County councillor for Glamorgan. JP. "An advanced Liberal, in favour of Home Rule, Disestablishment, etc." (1895). Leg amputated in accident (Information from the Rev. I. T. Rees). Of 4 Victoria Street, London, and Maes-y-gwernen Hall, Swansea Valley.

Deacon of Independent church (I. T. Rees). Member of Congregational Union committee from 1894 (*CYB*, 1894, p. xiii).
WWBMP 2.

Sir WILLIAM HENRY WILLS
1 Sept. 1830 - 29 Jan. 1911
MP (L) for Coventry, 1880-85
Bristol, E, Mar. 1895-1900

Tobacco manufacturer; chairman of W.D. and H. O. Wills and Sons. Head of richest family in Bristol (Meller, p. 68). Director of Great Western Railway, Phoenix Assurance Co. and Bristol Water Works Co. Chairman of Bristol Chamber of Commerce from 1863. Chairman of Provincial Water Companies Association. Mill Hill School, where captain; University College, London. Member of Bristol town council, 1862-80. High Sheriff of Bristol, 1877-78; and of Somerset, 1905-06. Unsuccessful candidate for Essex, SE, 1885, and Bristol, S, 1892. Dissenting Deputy. Interested in prison reform and reformatory schools. Trustee of Bristol municipal charities. Governor of Bristol Grammar School. Pro-Chancellor of University of Bristol from 1909. President of Bristol Fine Arts Academy. Gave money for Bristol Art Gallery, employing cousin as architect (Meller, p. 69) and a public library. Erected statue of Edmund Burke, sometime MP for Bristol, 1894. Governor of Sion Hospital. Fellow of Royal Geographical Society. Bart, 1893. Baron Winterstoke of Blagdon, 1906. JP, DL. Yachtsman. Of 25 Hyde Park Gardens, London; Blagdon, Somerset; and St Lawrence-on-Sea, Thanet.

His mother Mary was daughter of Robert Steven of Camberwell, a founder of LMS and British and Foreign Bible Society. Deacon of Highbury Congregational Church, Bristol. Trustee of Memorial Hall, 1872. Supported Mansfield College, 1886. Gave organ to Mill Hill School, 1898. Gave £1,000 to buy new site for Shaftesbury Mission in St Philip's area sponsored by Redland Park Congregational Church, opened 1909 (William Edwards, *Redland Park Congregational Church, Bristol* (Bristol, 1941), p. 77).

ODNB (acknowledging Congregational role). *WWW* 1897-1916. *WWBMP* 2. H. E. Meller, *Leisure and the Changing City, 1870-1914* (London, 1976).

JOHN WILSON
1828 - 29 Dec. 1905
MP (L) for Lanarkshire, Govan, Jan. 1889-1900

Iron tube manufacturer; head of John Wilson and Son, Oxford Street, Glasgow, and Govan. Paisley High School. JP, DL. " 'A Radical', and supports Home Rule for Ireland, 'and Scotland also'; in favour of popular control of the liquor traffic, religious equality, taxation of feu duties and ground rents, and free education, compulsorily administered, if necessary" (1900). Of Hillhead House, Glasgow.

Thought to be Congregationalist (*Christian Life*, 20 Aug. 1892, p. 399). Laid foundation stone of Morison Memorial Evangelical Union Church, Dumbarton Road, Clydebank, 3 Oct. 1896. (www.theclydebankstory. com/image.php?inum=TCSA00181). This church formed 1893 (Escott, p. 322), and so probably not Wilson's own. But because outside his constituency, he was probably member of Evangelical Union.
WWBMP 2.

HENRY SELFE PAGE WINTERBOTHAM
2 Mar. 1837 - 13 Dec. 1873
MP (L) for Stroud, Aug. 1867 - Dec. 1873

Barrister. Amersham School, University College, London, where LLD, 1859. Called to bar, Lincoln's Inn, 1860. Made initial impact on Commons by speech on university tests abolition. Under-Secretary of State for the Home Department, 1871. Died in Rome, where buried in Protestant Cemetery. "Parliament, the Liberal party, & especially the nonconforming part of the Liberal party, suffer a serious loss in his removal" (W. E. Gladstone to H. B. W. Brand, 29 Dec. 1873, in *The Gladstone Diaries,* Vol. 8, ed. H. C. G. Matthew (Oxford, 1982), pp. 431-2).

Member of Bedford Street Congregational Church, Stroud (*Stroud Journal,* 20 Dec. 1873, p. 2). Grandson of William Winterbotham, minister of Shortwood Baptist Church, Nailsworth, Gloucestershire. Henry's father, Lindsay, a banker, was a member of Shortwood until 1853, when his name was erased on his departure to Tewkesbury. Henry's name did not appear in the Shortwood records. (Information from W. O. Wicks). In London, Henry was a hearer of William Brock and a donor to Bloomsbury Baptist Church (G. W. M'Cree, *William Brock, D.D.: First Pastor of Bloomsbury Chapel* (London, 1876), p. 56; JCGB), although he sometimes also sat under Thomas Jones at Bedford Chapel, Oakley Square (*CYB,* 1883, p. 294). He was said to be a member of Brixton Independent Church under Baldwin Brown (JCGB).

ODNB. WWBMP.

WILLIAM WOODALL
15 Mar. 1832 - 8 Apr. 1901
MP (L) for Stoke-upon-Trent, 1880-85
Hanley, 1885-1900

Potter; senior partner of James Macintyre and Co., Burslem. Chairman of Sneyd Colliery Co. Manager of Burslem Gas Co. Crescent Schools, Liverpool. Chief bailiff of Burslem. Founded Woodall Liberal Club at Burslem. Chairman of Burslem School Board, 1870-80. President of Municipal Corporations Association. President of N Staffs Association of Mining and Mechanical Engineers. Secretary of Wedgwood Memorial Institute, providing additional wing. Presented free library to Burslem, bequeathing pictures to art gallery. Chairman of the N Staffs Committee for Promoting the Welfare of the Deaf and Dumb. Member of committee of Liberation Society. Chairman of Dissenting Deputies, 1899-1901 (Manning, p. 487). Surveyor-General of Ordnance, 1886. Financial Secretary to War Office, 1892-95. Advocate of disestablishment, local veto and votes for "duly qualified" women (1900), becoming chairman of the Central Committee for Women's Suffrage. Proposed amendment to 1884 Reform Bill in favour of female suffrage, losing by 271 to 135. Introduced women's suffrage bills, 1887, 1889 and 1891. Member of Royal Commissions on Technical Education (1881-84) and the Care of the Blind and Deaf Mutes (1886-89). JP. Chevalier of the Legion of Honour. Published *Paris after Two Sieges* (1872). Of Bleak House, Burslem.

Member of Burslem Congregational Church, which took the name Woodall Memorial and placed a bust of him on its façade in 1906. Member of Congregational Union committee (*CYB*, 1885, p. xvii; 1897, p. xiii).

ODNB (omitting religion except for posthumous church building). *WWW* 1897-1916. *WWBMP* 2. *Congregationalist*, Dec. 1882, pp. 953-5.

JOSEPH WOODHEAD
1824 - 21 May 1913
MP (L) for Yorkshire, West Riding, E, Spen Valley, 1885-92

Woollen manufacturer, later proprietor and editor of *Huddersfield Examiner*. Town councillor and alderman of Huddersfield; twice mayor. Freeman of Huddersfield, 1898. Retired voluntarily from Spen Valley, 1892, but unsuccessful at Huddersfield, Feb. 1893. Of 14 Craven Street, London.

Quaker origins. Member of Lane Chapel, Holmfirth; Ramsden Street Congregational Chapel, Huddersfield; and Milton Congregational Church, Huddersfield (JCGB).

WWBMP 2.

FRANK ASH YEO
18 Aug. 1832 - 4 Mar. 1888
MP (L) for Glamorgan, Gower, 1885 - Mar. 1888

Colliery proprietor. Educated in Bideford, Germany and France. Joined commercial staff of Cory, Sons & Co., Swansea, 1854. Partner, Cory, Yeo & Co., sinking Penrhiwceiber Colliery, then deepest mine in Wales. Chairman, Swansea Bank. Chairman, Swansea Harbour Trust, 1874-86. Member of Swansea town council, alderman and mayor, 1874 and 1886. JP. Of Sketty Hall, Swansea.

Deacon of Walter Road Congregational Church, Swansea (Information from the Rev. I. T. Rees). *WWBMP* 2.

Supplementary List of Supposed Congregational MPs

GEORGE ARMITSTEAD
28 Feb. 1824 - 7 Dec. 1915
MP (L) for Dundee, 1868 - Aug. 1873, 1880-85

Merchant trading with Russia. Born in Riga. Educated Wiesbaden and Heidelberg. Senior partner of Armitstead and Co., London, and George Armitstead and Co., Dundee. Lived in Dundee from 1848, but his English was still poor: he lacked the "ability to pronounce it with some approach to accuracy" (Michael St John, *The Demands of the People: Dundee Radicalism, 1850-1870* (Dundee, 1997), pp. 6, 54, quoting *Dundee Courier and Argus,* 20 Nov. 1868). Burgess of Dundee in right of his wife Jane, daughter of Edward Baxter, 1854. JP, DL, FRGS. Created Baron Armitstead, 19 July 1906. Died childless and barony became extinct. Candidate in 1857, standing for ballot and against Maynooth and Puseyism (I. G. C. Hutchison, *A Political History of Scotland, 1832-1924* (Edinburgh, 1986), p. 82). Favoured county government and shorter parliaments (1885). Of Kinloch Laggan, Kingussie, Inverness-shire.

United Presbyterian (I. G. C. Hutchison, *A Political History of Scotland, 1832-1924* (Edinburgh, 1986), p. 82). But wife's father became member of Ward Chapel, Dundee, 21 Aug. 1834 (W. D. McNaughton, *Early Congregational Independency in Lowland Scotland* (Glasgow, 2005), Vol. 1, p. 545). Regular worshipper at Westminster Chapel (*CW,* 12 Oct. 1903, p. 3). Donor to Cheshunt College, Cambridge (JCGB).

WWBMP. www.thepeerage.com.

ALFRED BILLSON
18 Apr. 1839 - 9 July 1907
MP (L) for Devon, NW, 1892-95
Halifax, Mar. 1897-1900
Staffordshire, NW, 1906-07

Solicitor, partner in Oliver Jones, Billson and Co., and joint proprietor of *Liverpool Daily Post.* Secretary of South-West Lancashire Liberal Association, 1866-84, and of Liverpool Liberal Association. President of Shropshire Liberal Association. Unsuccessful candidate in Devon, NW, 1895; Bradford, E, 1896; Halifax, 1900. Bibliophile. JP. Awarded knighthood in 1907 but died before it was gazetted. Son attended Eton and Magdalen College, Oxford. Of Rowton Castle, Shrewsbury, and 5 Cook Street, Liverpool.

Attender of Pembroke Chapel, Liverpool, prior to 1867 (Augustine Birrell,

Things Past Redress (London, 1937), p. 49). His law partner Isaac Oliver Jones and his son George Oliver Jones were Congregationalists (JCGB). Charles Silvester Horne spoke at Billson's funeral (*BW*, 18 July 1907, p. 35). Thought to be Congregationalist (*CW*, 4 Jan. 1906, p. vii), but allegiance doubtful.

WWW 1897-1916. Papers at Liverpool Record Office.

Sir THOMAS CHAMBERS
17 Dec. 1814 - 24 Dec. 1891
MP (L) for Hertford, 1852-57
Marylebone, 1865-85

Barrister. Admitted to Clare College, Cambridge, in 1837, but failed to graduate until 1846, when took LLB. Called to bar of Middle Temple, 1840; bencher, 1861; treasurer, 1872. QC., 1861. Common Sergeant of City of London, 1857-78. Recorder of City of London, 1878-91. Steward of Southwark, 1884-91. President of national chamber of trade, 1874 - *c.* 1880. Knight, 1872. DL. Defeated at Hertford, 1857. Advocate of permitting marriage with deceased wife's sister. Sabbatarian, opponent of liquor trade, favoured inspection of convent laundries. Opponent of centralisation. Co-author of *The Laws relating to Buildings* (1845); and *A Treatise on the Law of Railway Companies* (1848). Of 63 Gloucester Place, Portman Square, London.

Thought to be Independent on first election (*Eclectic Review*, Sept. 1852, p. 381), but degree rules it out. He had presumably recently shed earlier scruples that delayed his graduating. Buried in family vault in All Saints' Church, Hertford.

ODNB. WWBMP. Boase.

JOHN FREDERICK CHEETHAM
1835 - 25 Feb. 1916
MP (L) for Derbyshire, N, 1880-85
Stalybridge, Jan. 1905 - Jan. 1910

Cotton manufacturer. Son of John S. Cheetham. University College, London. Director of Manchester and Liverpool District Bank and of Ashton Gas Company. Member of Stalybridge School Board for 10 years. President of Stalybridge Mechanics' Institute. Governor of Owens College, Manchester. Built Stalybridge Public Library, 1897-1901. Hon. Freeman of Stalybridge, 1897. Alderman of Cheshire CC. Defeated at Derbyshire, High Peak, 1885 and 1892; Bury, 1895; Stalybridge, 1900. Narrowly defeated in 1885 after having been accused by Vicar of Hope of atheism

(*Buxton Advertiser,* 14 Nov. 1885, *per* JCGB). JP. PC, 1911. Fond of foreign travel and enjoyed climbing, making annual visit to the Alps. Left home and art collection to town. (www.tameside.gov.uk/leisure/new/jf_cheetham.htm). Of Eastwood, Stalybridge.

Associated with Stalybridge Congregational Church (*LN*, vol. 5, p. 322), but not identified as member. Married Beatrice Emma Astley at St Margaret's, Westminster, 1887, and so perhaps out of Congregational orbit. Yet laid foundation stone of Congregational Sunday school, 1905, giving £1,000 (website, as above).

WWW 1916-1928. *WWBMP* 2.

Sir SAVILLE BRINTON CROSSLEY
14 June 1857 - 25 Feb. 1935
MP (L) for Suffolk, N, 1885-86; (LU), 1886-92
MP (LU) for Halifax, 1900-06

Carpet manufacturer; chairman of J. Crossley and Sons Ltd. Son of Sir Francis Crossley. Eton and Balliol College, Oxford. Paymaster-General, 1902-05. Chairman of Liberal Unionist Council. Defeated at Halifax, Mar. 1897, and 1906; and at Islington (as Unionist), W, Jan. 1910. Succeeded as Bart.,1872. PC, 1902. MVO, 1902. KCVO, 1909. GCVO, 1922. Served in Boer War as captain then lieut.-colonel, Imperial Yeomanry. Colonel commanding P. W. O. Norfolk Artillery. JP, DL. High Sheriff of Suffolk, 1896. Lord Somerleyton, 1916. Lord in Waiting and whip in Lords, 1918-23. Hon. Secretary, King Edward's Hospital Fund. Chairman of Saturday Hospital Fund until 1914. Of Somerleyton Hall, Suffolk.

Listed as Free Churchman (*FCYB*, 1905, p. 285). But Anglican as adult.

WWW 1929-1940. *WWBMP* 2.

WILLIAM REES MORGAN DAVIES
11 May 1863 - 14 Apr. 1939
MP (L) for Pembrokeshire, 1892-98

Barrister. Son of Sir William Davies, MP, succeeding him in the seat. Eton and Trinity Hall, Cambridge. Called to bar, Inner Temple, 1887. Private Secretary to Sir William Harcourt, 1893-98. Supported disestablishment and Newcastle programme (1897). QC. Attorney-General for the Bahamas, 1898-1902. King's Advocate, Cyprus, 1902-07. Attorney-General for Hong Kong, 1907-12. Chief Justice of Hong Kong, 1912-24. Knight, 1913. JP, DL. Of 17 Pall Mall, London; and Scoveston, Milford Haven, Pembs.

No indication of religious affiliation, and, in particular, no evidence for Congregational allegiance.

WWW 1929-1940. *WWBMP* 2.

Sir CULLING EARDLEY EARDLEY (later EARDLEY SMITH)
21 Apr. 1805 - 21 May 1863
MP (L) for Pontefract, 1830-31
Bart, succeeding 1829. Interested in poor law reform in 1830s. Unsuccessful candidate for Pontefract, 1837; Edinburgh, 1846; and West Riding, 1848. Replaced "Smith" with "Eardley" in 1847. Eton and Oriel College, Oxford, not taking degree for conscientious reasons. Chairman and treasurer of Evangelical Voluntary Church Association, 1839. Chairman of Anti-Maynooth committee and conference, 1845. First chairman of council, president and treasurer of Evangelical Alliance from 1846. Defended religious liberty abroad.
Became convinced Evangelical after leaving Oxford. Inclined to Nonconformity but attended Evangelical parish churches. President of Hertfordshire Union of Independents and Baptists, 1842, 1856; treasurer, 1842-45. (Surman) Treasurer of LMS, 1844-63. Published revised version of Prayer Book, shorn of material offensive to Nonconformists, 1854.
ODNB. BDEB. Correspondence and papers, Hertfordshire Archives and Library Service.

Sir JOHN EASTHOPE
29 Oct. 1784 - 11 Dec. 1865
MP (L) for St Albans, 1826-30
Banbury, 1831
Leicester, 1837-47
Stockbroker from 1818, making £150,000 in a few years. Chief proprietor of *Morning Chronicle*, 1837-47. Chairman of London and South Western Railway. Director of the Canada Land Co. Chairman of the Mexican Mining Co. Son of Thomas Easthope of Tewkesbury. Advocate of abolition of church rates. Supported Graham's Factory Bill education clauses, 1843. Supported Anti-Corn Law League. Unsuccessful candidate for St Albans, 1821; Southampton, 1835; Lewes, Apr. 1837; and Bridgnorth, 1847. "[O]f Liberal opinions, gave no pledges" (1847). JP. Bart, 1841. Of Firgrove, near Weybridge, Surrey.
Attended Whetstone Congregational Chapel, Leics. His son, John (1810-49), was at Mill Hill School, 1820-23. (JCGB).
ODNB (without mention of religion). *WWBMP.* A. T. Patterson, *Radical Leicester* (Leicester, 1954). Correspondence and papers, Duke University, NC, USA.

SYDNEY EVERSHED
1825 - 8 Nov. 1903
MP (L) for Staffordshire, Burton, Aug. 1886-1900

Brewer from 1853. Private school of the Rev. E. Kell, Newport, Isle of Wight. Alderman of Burton-on-Trent; twice mayor. Commissioner of taxes. Supported land and poor law reform, old age pensions in connection with friendly societies, cottage and allotment improvements (1900). JP. Recreations: farming, fishing, shooting. Of Albury House, Burton-on-Trent.

"Mr. Evershed had a leaning towards Unitarianism, but was often to be seen at church and chapel" (*Staffordshire Advertiser*, 14 Nov. 1903, supplement). Two of his sons were at Amersham Hall School in 1880s. Related to Cozens-Hardy family. According to Basil Cozens-Hardy, left Congregationalism over drink issue. Perhaps once member of Congregational Church, but said to be member of George Street United Methodist Free Church, Burton-on-Trent (JCGB).

WWW 1897-1916. *WWBMP.*

JOHN LAWRENCE GANE
1837 - Feb./Mar. 1895
MP (L) for Leeds, E, 1886 - Feb./Mar. 1895

Barrister. Son of Edward Gane and Caroline, daughter of Joseph Lawrence of Freshford, Somerset. Dissenters' School, Taunton. Married Elizabeth, daughter of George Dowse of Worlon, Wilts. Called to bar, Middle Temple, 1870. QC, 1885. Unsuccessful candidate at Leeds, E, 1885. Undertook voyage in company of Lord Randolph Churchill for health reasons, but died at sea on return journey from New Zealand.

Nonconformist (*CW*, 4 July 1895, p. 528). Possibly Congregationalist? *WWBMP* 2.

CHARLES HINDLEY
25 June 1796 - 1 Dec. 1857
MP (L) for Ashton-under-Lyne, 1835-57

Cotton spinner, Dukinfield. President of Ashton-under-Lyne Mechanics' Institute, 1825-57. Urged enfranchisement of Ashton in Reform Bill, 1831 (W. M. Bowman, *England in Ashton-under-Lyne* (Ashton-under-Lyne, 1960), p. 640). Defeated at Ashton, 1832; and at Warrington, 1835. Returned unopposed, 1847, 1852, 1857. Supported restriction of factory hours, but his mill prosecuted for excessive hours, 1834 and 1836. One of 6 MPs who signed Charter, 1837. President of Peace Society, presiding at first International Peace Congress in London: "peace, economy and reform were his watchwords" (1853). Supporter of Lord's Day Observance Society, Health of Towns Association, Metropolitan Drapers' Association and Ragged Schools Union. Of Portland House, Ashton; and subsequently Dukinfield Lodge.

Moravian, commemorated at Fairfield Moravian Settlement, Droylsden. Moravian School, Fulneck, and studied privately with the Rev. C. A. Pohlman at Haverfordwest. Schoolteacher at Moravian School, Gracehill, Ireland. Intended to enter Moravian ministry until death of older brother in 1819 led him to return to manage the family's two cotton mills. Moravian "but usually associates with the Independents" (*Nonconformist*, 4 Aug. 1852, p. 597). Laid foundation stone of Westminster Chapel and of Park Chapel, Crouch End, in 1853 (JCGB).

ODNB. BDMBR 2. *WWBMP. BDEB.* Boase. James Grant, *Random Recollections of the House of Commons* (London, 1836), pp. 199-200. Michael Nevell, *People who made Tameside* (Tameside, 1994), pp. 31-6, 77.

JAMES HOWARD
  1821 - 25 Jan. 1889
  MP (L) for Bedford, 1868-74
  MP (L) for Bedfordshire, 1880-85

  Agricultural implement maker; proprietor of Britannia Works, Bedford. Chairman of Bedford and Northampton Railway. Son of John Howard, JP, of Cauldwell, Bedford. Bedford Public Schools. High Sheriff of Bedfordshire, 1878. JP, DL. Author of *Continental Farming and Peasantry* (1870); *The History of Steam Ploughing*, etc. Of Clapham Park, Bedford.

  Nonconformist (*CW*, 4 July 1895, p. 528). Probably Methodist (JCGB).

  WWBMP.

JOHN HUSBAND
  1839-
  MP (L) for Wiltshire, Cricklade, 1892-95

  Corn merchant. President of S Hackney Liberal and Radical Association. Favoured Newcastle programme (1895). Of Moreton Lodge, Upper Clapton, London.

  Congregationalist (*Christian Life and Unitarian Herald*, 20 Aug. 1892, p. 399), but that source unreliable and no further evidence found.

  WWBMP 2.

WILLIAM JACKS
  18 Mar. 1841 - 9 Aug. 1907
  MP (L) for Leith District, 1885-86
  Stirlingshire, 1892-95

Iron and steel merchant; senior partner of William Jacks and Co. from 1880, with Andrew Bonar Law as junior partner, 1885-98. President, Glasgow Chamber of Commerce, 1904-05; Council of Commercial College, Glasgow; British Iron Trade Association, 1896; West of Scotland Iron and Steel Institute. JP. LLD, Glasgow, 1899. From Swinton, Berwickshire, entered Hartlepool shipyard, then Sunderland engine works. Moved to Glasgow, 1869. Opposed Home Rule, 1886, when replaced as Liberal candidate for Leith District by Gladstone. Unsuccessful LU candidate for Leith District, Aug. 1886. Subsequently became Home Ruler. Defeated in Stirlingshire, 1895. President of Glasgow literary, scientific and art clubs, lecturing on social, economic and literary subjects. Published translation of Lessing's *Nathan the Wise* (1894), *Robert Burns in Other Tongues* (1896), lives of Bismarck (1899), James Watt (1901) and the Emperor William II (1904). Left £20,000 to Glasgow University to found William Jacks chair of German language and literature. Of The Gart, Callendar, Perthshire.

Congregationalist (*Christian Life and Unitarian Herald*, 20 Aug. 1892, p. 399), but that source unreliable and no further evidence found.

ODNB (omitting religion). *WWBMP* 2. *WWW* 1897-1916.

Sir JOSEPH FRANCIS LEESE

28 Feb. 1845 - 29 July 1914

MP (L) for Lancashire, Accrington, 1892-1909

Barrister. University of London. Called to bar, Inner Temple, 1868. QC, 1891. Recorder of Manchester from 1893. Bencher of Inner Temple, 1898. Knight, 1895. Bart, 1908. Unsuccessfully contested Preston in 1868 and Accrington in 1886. Causes supported included Welsh and Scottish disestablishment, direct veto and eight hours (1909). Of Sutton Park Cottage, Surrey.

Born in a Baptist family and a lay student at Regent's Park College (*Freeman*, 22 July 1892, p. 516). At one time a member of Bowdon Downs Congregational Church, Manchester (H. Shaw, *The Story of the Church of Christ of the Congregational Order meting at Bowdon Downs, 1839-1900* (Manchester, 1900), p. 25). But not listed as Free Churchman in *FCYB*, 1905 or 1907, and so unlikely to have remained Congregationalist.

WWBMP 2. *WWW* 1897-1916.

REGINALD McKENNA

6 July 1863 - 6 Sept. 1943

MP (L) for Monmouthshire, N, 1895-1918

Barrister. King's College, London, and Trinity Hall, Cambridge. Called to bar, Inner Temple, 1887. Contested Clapham, 1892. Close to Sir Charles Dilke. Specialist in tariffs, founding Free Trade Union, 1903. Financial Secretary to the Treasury, 1905. President of Board of Education, 1907-08, failing to satisfy Nonconformist claims. First Lord of the Admiralty, 1908-11. Home Secretary, 1911-15, steering Welsh Disestablishment Bill. Chancellor of the Exchequer, 1915-16. Defeated in Pontypool, 1918. Chairman of Midland Bank from 1919. Author of *Post-War Banking Policy* (1928). Of 36 Smith Square, Westminster.

Father was Roman Catholic from Monaghan, converting to Protestantism. Reginald "identified himself as a Congregationalist" (*ODNB*). Not in list of Free Churchmen published in *CW*, 1 Feb. 1906, p. 5, but added 8 Feb. 1906, p. 4, after newspaper had enquired. His wife Pamela a member of King's Weigh House in 1920s (JCGB).

Stephen McKenna, *Reginald McKenna,1863-1943: A Memoir* (London, 1948). *ODNB. WWBMP* 2.

Sir WILLIAM MATHER
15 July 1838 - 18 Sept. 1920
MP (L) for Salford, S, 1885-86
Lancashire, Gorton, Mar. 1889-95
Lancashire, Rossendale, Feb. 1900 - Mar. 1904

Ironmaster; chairman of Mather and Platt Ltd, supplying equipment for textile mills. Founded Chloride Electrical Storage Co., 1891, and Castner-Kellner Co. Ltd, 1895, manufacturing batteries, chlorine and caustic soda. Member of Institute of Mechanical Engineers. Vice-president of British Engineers' Association. First president of Association of Technical Associations, 1894. Frequently visited Russia. Provided evening science school from 1873 at Salford Iron Works, and introduced eight hour day, 1893. Member of council of Owens College and Victoria University, establishing department of Russian. Knight of Francis Joseph Order of Austria, 1873. Reported on technical education in America and Russia for royal commission, 1883. Chairman of Froebel Educational Institute of London. Member of committee on reorganisation of War Office, 1902. Trustee of Gordon College, Khartoum. President of British Science Guild and Textile Institute. Chairman of British education section of Franco-British Exhibition, 1908. JP. LLD, Manchester, 1908. Knight, 1902. PC, 1910. Of Woodhill House, Prestwich.

Reputed to be Congregationalist (*Christian Life and Unitarian Herald,* 20 Aug. 1892, p. 399), but no evidence found. School at Accrington under

Rev. Dr Badley, Swedenborgian. Married Emma Jane Watson of Highbury at Swedenborgian chapel, Argyle Square, London. Buried at Prestwich parish church.

L. E. Mather, *The Right Honourable Sir William Mather, 1838-1920* (London, [1925]). *ODNB* (containing nothing on Congregationalism). *WWBMP* 2. *WWW* 1916-1928.

CHARLES MORLEY
1847 - 27 Oct. 1917
MP (L) for Breconshire, 1895-1906

Partner in I. and R. Morley. Director of Holborn Viaduct Land Co. Trinity College, Cambridge. Unsuccessful candidate for Somerset, E, 1892. Hon Secretary to Royal College of Music. Of 46 Bryanston Square, London, and Shockerwick House, Bath.

Son of Samuel Morley, maintaining several of father's Congregational trusteeships and benefactions (*BDMBR* 2, p. 362). Trustee of King's Weigh House, 1885-1910 (JCGB). Listed as Free Churchman (*FCYB*, 1905, p. 286), but Anglicans officiated at his funeral (JCGB).

WWW 1916-1928. *WWBMP* 2. C. A. M. Press, *Liberal Leaders of Somerset* (Bridgwater, 1890), pp. 62-72 (without reference to religion).

Sir GEORGE NEWNES
13 Mar. 1851 - 9 June 1910
MP (L) for Cambridgeshire, E, 1885-95
Swansea Town, 1900 - Jan. 1910
Newspaper owner; founder of *Westminster Gazette* (1892); proprietor of *Tit-bits* (1881) *Strand Magazine* (1891) etc. Silcoates School; Shireland Hall, Birmingham; and City of London School. Bart, 1895. JP. Defeated for Cambridgeshire, E, 1895. Suffered from alcoholism from mid-1890s. Gave library to Putney and cable railway to Matlock and Lynton. Of Wildcroft, Putney Heath, SW.
Son of T. M. Newnes, minister of Glenorchy Chapel, Matlock Bath. Married Priscilla, daughter of the Rev. James Hillyard. Religious scruples would not allow him to use methods of *News of the World*, and so forced to sell *Weekly Dispatch* at a loss (*ODNB*). Presented R. J. Campbell with car (*CW*, 8 Feb. 1906, p. 3). Not Congregationalist in later life (Surman).
Hulda Friederichs, *The Life of Sir George Newnes* (London, 1911). *ODNB* (containing nothing explicit about religious allegiance). *WWW* 1897-1916.

Sir THOMAS WILLANS NUSSEY
12 Oct. 1868 - 12 Oct. 1947
MP (L) for Pontefract, June 1893 - Dec. 1910

Barrister. Leamington School and Trinity Hall, Cambridge. Called to bar, Inner Temple, 1893. JP, DL. Bart, 1909. Contested Maidstone, 1892. Of Rushwood, East Tanfield, Ripon, Yorks.

Baptism recorded by Headingley Hill Congregational Church, Leeds. His father Thomas was a seatholder there and on finance committee in 1867, but not apparently a member. (JCGB). Not in list of Free Church MPs in *FCYB*, 1905 or 1907.

WWBMP 2.

JAMES ALLANSON PICTON
8 Aug. 1832 - 4 Feb. 1910
MP (L) for Leicester, June 1884 - Aug. 1894

Minister and journalist. Liverpool Institute; Owens College, Manchester; London University MA in classics. Lancashire Independent College while at Owens College. Minister of Cheetham Hill Congregational Church, Manchester, 1857-62; of Gallowtree Gate Congregational Church, Leicester, 1862-69; and of St Thomas' Square Congregational Church, Hackney, 1869-79. Gave Sunday afternoon lectures to working men at Manchester and Leicester. President of Leicester Literary and Philosophical Society. Opposed compulsory vaccination. Member of London School Board, 1870-79; and of Caernarvonshire CC and its Local Education Committee to 1909. Member of royal commission on market rights and tolls, 1888. For 20 years regular political leader writer on *CW* until his residence in Wales made it impossible. (*CW*, 10 Feb. 1910, p. 4, whose dates of pastorates have been preferred). Supported kindergartens, phonetic teaching of reading and Froebel philosophy of education. Learned Welsh. JP. Of 80 Regent's Park Road, London.

Influenced towards liberal theology by A. J. Scott, principal of Owens College from 1851. Went to Halle, Heidelberg, Leipzig, returning to defend Samuel Davidson of Lancashire College, 1856. In 1869 introduced liturgical services without full support of members at St Thomas'. Addressed Leicester Conference on Religious Communion in 1877 on "Some Relations of Theology to Religion", arguing that varied theologies were aids to the religious life (Mark Hopkins, *Nonconformity's Romantic Generation* (Carlisle, 2004), p. 90). At Congregational Union spring assembly 1878 made farewell speech to organised Congregationalism. Became Spinozan pantheist. Later lectured at South Place Ethical Society,

Finsbury, and addressed Hampstead Ethical Society, 1901. Author of *New Theories and the Old Faith* (1870), *The Mystery of Matter* (1873), *Oliver Cromwell: The Man and his Mission* (1882), *Lessons from the Rise and Fall of the English Commonwealth* (1884), *The Conflict of Oligarchy and Democracy* (1885), *The Religion of Jesus* (1893), *Sir James A. Picton: A Biography* (1891), *The Religion of the Universe* (1904), *Spinoza: A Handbook to the Ethics* (1907), *Man and the Bible: A Review of the Place of the Bible in Human History* (1909); etc.

ODNB. WWW, 1897-1916. *WWBMP* 2.

JAMES ROWLANDS
1 Oct. 1851 - 1 Mar. 1920
MP (L) for Finsbury, E, 1886-95
Kent, NW, 1906 - Jan. 1910, Dec. 1910 - Mar. 1920

Watchcase maker. Working Men's College, Great Ormond Street. Secretary of Finsbury branch of London Municipal Reform League. Freeman of Goldsmiths' Company. President of Gas Consumers' Protection League, 1893. Secretary of Leasehold Enfranchisement Association. Member of London School Board. Hon. secretary of Land Law Reform Association. Unsuccessful candidate at Finsbury, E, 1885 and 1895; and in Kent, NW, Jan. 1910. Of 119 Mercer's Road, Tufnell Park, London.

Congregationalist according to *BW,* 18 May 1888, p. 50. But no claims of Nonconformist allegiance by press in 1906 parliament.

WWW 1916-1928. *WWBMP* 3.

JONATHAN SAMUEL
1853 - 22 Feb. 1917
MP (L) for Stockton-on-Tees, 1895-1900, Jan. 1910-17

In iron and steel trades, then grocer. Member of Stockton-on-Tees council (1882-1904) and alderman from 1896; mayor, 1894-95 and 1902. Freeman of Stockton, 1904. Member (from 1889) and alderman (from 1903) of Durham CC. Member of Tees Conservancy Board, 1893-1904. Defeated at Stockton, 1900. JP. Of 23 Lorne Terrace, Stockton.

Congregationalist according to *CW*, 27 Sept. 1900, p. 3, but member of Stockton-on-Tees Baptist Tabernacle (*Baptist Times*, 16 Dec. 1910, p. 822). *WWWBMP* 2.

WILLIAM RAWSON SHAW
1860 - 14 Apr. 1932
MP (L) for Halifax, Feb. 1893 - *c.* Feb. 1897

Son of Thomas Shaw. Rugby; Trinity College, Cambridge. Lieutenant in 2nd W Yorkshire Yeomanry Cavalry (Prince of Wales' Own). For three years private secretary to Professor James Stuart, MP. President of Stainland Liberal Association from its start. Member of W Sussex CC. JP. Of Stonygate, Halifax, and Oakes House, Stainland, Yorks.

CW, 18 July 1895, p. 558, and JCGB doubtful about Congregational allegiance.

WWBMP 2.

SAMUEL STOREY
13 Jan. 1841 - 18 Jan. 1925
MP (L) for Sunderland, Apr. 1881-95
MP (Independent Tariff Reform) for Sunderland, Jan. 1910 - Dec. 1910

Proprietor of *Sunderland Echo*; founder and chief proprietor of *Tyneside Daily Echo*. St Andrew's Parish Church School, Newcastle-upon-Tyne; Durham Diocesan Training School for Masters. Master at Birtley C. of E. School, 1860-64. Manager of Atlas Permanent Building Society, 1865-71. Partner in Armstrong, Addison and Co., timber merchants, Sunderland, 1876-81. Member of Sunderland town council from 1869; alderman from 1877; mayor, 1876, 1877 and 1880. Secured Nonconformist co-operation to gain control of Sunderland School Board (1877-85), on which he sat, 1877-83. Alderman of Durham CC, 1892-98, 1907-13; councillor, 1898-1907; chairman, 1894-97, 1898-1905. Hon. secretary and treasurer of N Durham Liberal Registration Association, 1874-85. President of Houghton-le-Spring Liberal Association. Republican, denouncing royal grants in Commons. In partnership with Andrew Carnegie to run chain of radical and republican newspapers, 1882-85. Vice-president of People's League for the Abolition of the House of Lords, 1884. Member of Royal Commission on the Depression of Trade, 1885-86. Supported eight hours movement. Unsuccessful at Sunderland, 1895; and at Newcastle, 1900. Resigned as chairman of Northern Liberal Fedeation, 1903, because accepted tariff reform. JP, DL. Freeman of Sunderland, 1921. Of Southill, Chester-le-Street, and Paxton House, Berwickshire.

Thought to be Congregationalist (*CW*, 27 Sept. 1900, p. 13). But apparently Anglican in early years and not listed as defeated Nonconformist, 1895 (*CW*, 18 July 1895, p. 538). A Free Methodist according to Geoffrey Milburn, *Religion in Sunderland in the Mid-Nineteenth Century* (Sunderland, 1983), p. 53.

Patricia J. Storey, "Samuel Storey of Sunderland (1841-1925): His Life and Career as a Local Politician and a Newspaper Proprietor up to

1895", Edinburgh MLitt, 1978. *BDMBR* 2 (omitting religion, except as above). *WWW* 1916-1928. *WWBMP* 2.

JAMES STUART

2 Jan. 1843 - 13 Oct. 1913
MP (L) for Hackney, Nov. 1884-1885
Shoreditch, Hoxton, 1885-1900
Sunderland, 1906-Jan. 1910

Professor of Mechanism and Applied Mechanics, Cambridge University, 1875-89. Madras School, St Andrews. St Andrews University and Trinity College, Cambridge, where became fellow, 1866. Associate of Institute of Civil Engineers. Lord Rector of St Andrews University, 1899-1901. LLD (St Andrews), 1875. Promoter of university extension teaching from 1867. First secretary of Cambridge local lectures syndicate, 1873-76. Editor of *Star* and *Morning Leader*, 1890-98. Alderman of London CC, 1889-98; elected member, 1901-07. PC, 1909. Unsuccessful candidate at Cambridge University, Nov. 1882, at Hoxton, 1900, and at Sunderland, Jan. 1910. Prominent supporter of anti-Contagious Diseases Acts movement. In favour of female suffrage and reform of House of Lords. Director of J. and J. Colman, mustard manufacturers, from 1898. Chairman of governors, King Edward VI Grammar School, Norwich. Served on several royal commissions. Author of *A Chapter of Science* (1883); *A Lecture on Science and Revelation*, 2nd edn (1872); *Principles of Christianity* (1888); etc. Of 24 Grosvenor Road, London; and Carrow Abbey, Norwich.

Family from Falkland Congregational Church, Fife, then Markinch Free Church of Scotland. At Cambridge, supported Castle End Mission (Congregational) but in 1879 petitioned for a Presbyterian church there. (JCGB) Marriage to Laura Elizabeth, daughter of J. J. Colman, 1890, at Prince's Street Congregational Church, Norwich, conducted by its minister, G. S. Barrett, and R. W. Dale. "I have heard a great many sermons by Dr. Barrett of Norwich, and I never heard him preach a bad one. Dr. Dale . . . illuminated every subject he touched, and was delightful friend, as well as an admirable speaker." (Stuart, *Reminiscences*, p. 262) No evidence of membership at Prince's Street (JCGB).

James Stuart, *Reminiscences*, privately printed (London, 1911). *ODNB* (omitting religion). *WWBMP*, 2. Correspondence, lectures and papers at Cambridge University Library.

WILLIAM SUMMERS

1853 - 1 Jan. 1893
MP (L) for Stalybridge, 1880-85
Huddersfield, 1886 - Jan. 1893

Barrister. Called to bar, Lincoln's Inn, 1881. Son of John Summers, iron manufacturer of Ashton-under-Lyne. Owens College, Manchester; University College, Oxford; and London University. Favoured "an active and orderly progress" (1892). Defeated at Stalybridge, 1885. Member of convocation of London University. Governor of Victoria University. Fellow of Statistical Society. Died in India. Of Ryecroft Hall, Audenshaw, Manchester.

Connected with Stalybridge Congregational Church (*LN*, Vol. 5, p. 322), but that suggests something less than membership.

WWBMP 2. Boase. *T*, 2 Jan. 1893, p. 5.

DAVID ALFRED THOMAS
26 Mar. 1856 - 3 July 1918
MP (L) for Merthyr Tydfil, Mar. 1888 - Jan. 1910
Cardiff District, 1910

Colliery proprietor and financier; managing director of Cambrian Collieries. Jesus and Gonville and Caius Colleges, Cambridge. Member of Ystradyfodwyg Board of Health after university. President of Cardiff Chamber of Commerce, 1895. President of S Wales Liberal Federation, 1893-97. President of Local Government Board, 1916-17. Minister of Food Control, 1917-18. Baron Rhondda, 1916; Viscount, 1918. JP, DL. Freemason. Of Llanwern, Newport, Mons.

Listed as Free Churchman (*FCYB*, 1907, p. 261), and thought to be Congregationalist. Parents attended Calfaria Welsh Baptist Chapel, Aberdare, to *c*. 1859, when moved to Carmel English Baptist Chapel and afterwards to Tabernacle English Congregational Church. Father Samuel Thomas then gave up attendance, reading sermons at home. "Brought up a strict Congregationalist, and retaining to the end of his life a special affection for the Congregational Church, which he believed to be broader than many others, he left college a confirmed agnostic" (Viscountess Rhondda *et al.*, *D. A. Thomas, Viscount Rhondda* (London, 1921), p. 32). But baptised in 1882 at St Andrew's Parish Church, near Barry, at twenty-six: "religion was a subject concerning which he spoke less than he thought" (Morgan, pp. 32-3). "I do not suppose that he himself exactly knew how much he did believe. Certain it is that he said his prayers every night and morning . . ." (Viscountess Rhondda, pp. 32-3). On his death, the widow summoned his first cousin, H. Arnold Thomas, minister of Highbury Congregational Church, Bristol, to hold a service in the presence of his body. "They told me", said Arnold Thomas, "that David cared a good deal about religion, and had said it would mean much more to him if he ever got better. The doctor said, 'But you don't mean psalm-singing and that kind of thing,' and the reply was, 'Yes, I do mean that.'" Nephew of David Thomas, previously minister of Highbury. (Nathaniel Micklem, *Arnold Thomas of Bristol* (London, 1925), p. 14) J. Vyrnwy Morgan, *Life of Viscount Rhondda* (London, 1918). *ODNB* (omitting religion). *WWW* 1916-1928. *WWBMP* 2. Papers at National Library of Wales.

GEORGE DONISTHORNE THOMPSON
18 June 1804 - 7 Oct. 1878
MP (L) for Tower Hamlets, 1847-52

Anti-slavery lecturer, visiting the United States, 1834-35. East India proprietor. Student of Grey's Inn, 1843. Favoured further free trade, ballot, short parliaments; opposed to ecclesiastical endowments (1852). Contested Southampton, Aug. 1842, and Tower Hamlets, 1852. Member of National Parliamentary Reform Association, and of Anti-Corn Law League. Took part in formation of British India Association, visiting India. Received freedom of Edinburgh, 1846. Majority in Tower Hamlets the greatest then on record; a poor man, whose last speech was at 1867 meeting to welcome Lloyd Garrison (J. Passmore Edwards, *A Few Footprints*, 2nd edn (London, 1906), p. 28). Of 128 Sloane Street, London.

Married daughter of Richard Spry, Countess of Huntingdon's Connexion minister, 1831. No other Congregational connection found.

ODNB (omitting religion). *WWBMP.* Boase. Papers at John Rylands University Library, Manchester.

JOSHUA WALKER
28 Sept. 1786 - 22 Jan. 1862
MP for Aldeburgh, 1818 - May 1829

Iron, steel and lead manufacturer. Inherited part of his father's share in family firm, Joshua Walker and Co., at Rotherham, 1815. Lived in London, supervising lead manufacturing, specially in Lambeth. Partner in banks in Sheffield, Rotherham and London from 1820s. Returned to parliament by his cousin Samuel for Aldeburgh, remaining until disagreement with his new patron, Marquess of Hertford, over Catholic emancipation, led to resignation.

Son of Joshua Walker (1750-1815), deacon of Masbrough Independent Chapel and founder of Rotherham Independent Academy (Thorne 5, p. 467). No evidence of Congregational membership found.

R. G. Thorne, *The House of Commons, 1790-1820*, 5 vols (London, 1986), 5, p. 467.

SAMUEL WALKER

4 Sept. 1779 - 30 Jan. 1851

MP for Aldeburgh, 1818-20

Iron, steel and lead manufacturer. Glasgow University. Captain, Rotherham Volunteer Infantry, 1798; Lieutenant-Colonel Commandant, 1804. Lieutenant-Colonel Commandant, Strafforth and Tickhill Regiment, West Yorkshire Militia, 1808. Before 1818 election, bought electoral interest in Aldeburgh, returning himself and Joshua. Did not speak in Commons or seek re-election, selling interest in 1822. After vicissitudes of firm, became bankrupt, 1832. Retired to Nether Stilton, near Northallerton.

Son of Samuel Walker (1742-92), cousin of Joshua Walker, MP. No evidence of Congregational membership found.

R. G. Thorne, *The House of Commons, 1790-1820*, 5 vols (London, 1986), 5, p. 467.

JOHN WHITWELL

6 Sept. 1812 - 28 Nov. 1880

MP (L) for Kendal, 1868 - Nov. 1880

Manufacturer of woollens and carpets. Mayor of Kendal six times. President of Kendal Chamber of Commerce and of National Association of Chambers of Commerce until death. Favoured revival of small tenements rating bill (1880). Lieutenant colonel of the Westmoreland Rifle Volunteers, 1869-80. Wrote *The Necessary Legislation for Incorporating Trades Societies*. Of Bank House, Kendal.

Reputed Congregationalist. Friends' School, Darlington. Married Anna Maud of Bradford by Quaker rites, 1836. In aftermath of Beacon controversy, dismissed from Quakers in 1840. While his brothers Isaac and Edward joined Zion Church, Kendal, which associated with Evangelical Union, though not actually in it, John joined parish church (*Kendal Mercury and Times*, 3 Dec. 1880). Hence not Congregationalist.

WWBMP. Boase. *T*, 29 Nov. 1880, p. 9; 3 Dec. 1880, p. 5.

THOMAS WHITWORTH

1844-1912

MP (L) for Drogheda, Mar. 1869-74

Cotton and commission merchant, Manchester; of Benjamin Whitworth and Brothers. Son of Benjamin Whitworth, replacing him on his disqualification from seat. A "general supporter of Mr. Gladstone's government, specially in his legislation on Irish matters" (1873). Composed MS account of "Personal Experiences of the House of Commons, Sessions 1869/74", showing that he never spoke and rarely attended after his first two sessions because of Manchester business commitments (Binfield, p. 132). Of Oakfield, Withington, near Manchester.

His wife, Elizabeth, the daughter of Robert Shaw, an Inghamite who became a Baptist, attended Anglican services in later life. Two of Thomas's sisters were members of Bowdon Downs Congregational Church. But no evidence of Congregational membership found and MS suggests "benignly lapsed dissent". (Binfield, pp. 127, 132, 134, quoted at p. 132).

J. C. G. Binfield, "The Shaping of a Dissenting Interest", in Stephen Taylor and David L. Wykes (eds), *Parliament and Dissent* (Edinburgh, 2005), pp. 126-34. *WWBMP.*

WILLIAM WHITWORTH
1814-
MP (L) for Newry, Feb. 1874-80

Merchant of Drogheda. Brother of Benjamin Whitworth. High Sheriff of Drogheda, 1869. JP. Of 11 Holland Park, London, and The Sycamores, Drogheda.

No evidence of Congregational membership found.

J. C. G. Binfield, "The Shaping of a Dissenting Interest", in Stephen Taylor and David L. Wykes (eds), *Parliament and Dissent* (Edinburgh, 2005), p. 133. *WWBMP.*

JOSEPH POWELL WILLIAMS
18 Nov. 1840 - 7 Feb. 1904
MP (L) for Birmingham, S, 1885-86
MP (LU) for Birmingham, S, 1886 - Feb. 1904

Post Office official and businessman. Proprietary school, Hagley Road, Birmingham, under Dr Badham. Entered offices of Graham and James, merchants of Ludgate Hill, London, and in America as representative of this and other firms at outbreak of Civil War. Appointed by Rowland Hill, father's cousin, to Post Office, where helped establish Post Office Savings Bank and became friend of Anthony Trollope, for whom he read proofs of works including *Phineas Finn.* Retired and returned to Birmingham, 1873. Chairman of Midland Railway Carriage and Waggon Co. Director of Scottish Union and National Insurance Co. Town councillor from 1877 for seven years; then alderman for four years. Chairman of Finance Committee for five years to 1886, issuing Corporation stock. JP. Hon. secretary, Birmingham Liberal Association. Hon. secretary, National Liberal Federation, writing pamphlets on it, including on county government and Ballot Act. Contributed article to *Nineteenth Century* on taxation of ground rents. Organised Liberal victory at Birmingham School Board election, 1884. Largely responsible for boundaries of Birmingham constituencies approved by Boundary Commissioners following 1885 Redistribution Act. Maiden speech in Commons, 31 Mar. 1886, moved second reading of bill to relieve certain boroughs of county rates. After LU split, chairman of executive of National Liberal Union. Vice-president of Birmingham Liberal Unionist Association. Chairman of Management Committee, Liberal Unionist Association, organising 1892 election campaign. Financial Secretary to War Office, 1895-1900. PC. Supported Joseph Chamberlain in tariff reform campaign, becoming chairman of Imperial Tariff Committee and sitting on council of Tariff Reform League. Played for Warwickshire County Cricket Club and for W. G. Grace's London County team; also played Rugby football. Of 6 Great George Street, Westminster; and Beckenham, Kent.

Regular attender of Carr's Lane Congregational Church during ministry of R. W. Dale, deriving inspiration for municipal and political work from him: "a friend and warm admirer of Dr. Dale" (*Birmingham Daily Post*, 8 Feb. 1904, p. 5). Funeral at General Cemetery, Key Hill, conducted by W. S. Houghton, minister of Francis Road Congregational Church, Birmingham (*Birmingham Daily Post*, 10 Feb. 1904, p. 11). No indication of membership found.

WWW, 1897-1916. *WWBMP*, 2. *Birmingham Daily Post*, 8 Feb. 1904, p. 5.

Sir FREDERICK WILLS
21 Nov. 1838 - 18 Feb. 1909
MP (LU) for Bristol, N, 1900-06

Tobacco manufacturer; director of W. D. and H. O. Wills Ltd. Independent College, Taunton, and Amersham School. Married, 1867, Anne, daughter of James Hamilton, D D, Presbyterian minister. Member of Bristol town council from 1885. Governor of Guy's Hospital. JP. Bart, 1897. LU candidate in Launceston, 1895 and 1898. Of 9 Kensington Park Gardens, London; Northmoor, near Dulverton, Devon; and Manor Heath, Bournemouth.

Baptised in Penn Street Calvinistic Methodist Chapel, Bristol. Cousin of W. H. Wills. (http://members.cox.net/ghgraham/frederickwills1838/html). No indication of Congregational membership found.

WWW 1897-1916. *WWBMP* 2.

HENRY JOSEPH WILSON
14 Apr. 1833 - 29 June 1914
MP (L) for Yorkshire, West Riding, S, Holmfirth, 1885-1912

Director of Sheffield Smelting Co. Dissenters' School, Taunton; University College, London, for year. Married Charlotte, daughter of Charles Cowan, MP for Edinburgh. Farmer near Mansfield, Notts, 1853-67. Organised Mansfield Mechanics' Institute. First president of Mansfield Co-operative Society. Joined brother in Sheffield firm, 1867. Brought Joseph Chamberlain to Sheffield as candidate, 1874. Secretary of Sheffield Liberal Association from 1875. Member of Sheffield School Board, 1876-87, 1891-93; vice-chairman, 1882; chairman, 1884. Supported anti-slavery and North in American Civil War. Supporter of Liberation Society. Attended inauguration of United Kingdom Alliance, 1853. Vice-president, then president, of British Temperance League. Secretary from 1872 of Northern Counties League for Abolition of Contagious Diseases Acts. Joint secretary from 1875 with Josephine Butler of British, Continental and General Federation for the Abolition of the Government Regulation of Prostitution. Promoted Indian National Vigilance Association from 1886. Member of India Office Committee on Regulation of Prostitution in India, 1893. Member of Royal Commission on Opium in India, 1893-95, producing minority report against the trade. JP. Supported 48-hour week from 1892. Pro-Boer. "A Radical, opposed to Aggressive Foreign Policy, Militarism, Protection, etc." (1912). Passive resister. Of Osgathorpe Hills, Sheffield.

Father's first wife Sarah was sister of Samuel Morley. Henry ran Sunday school for agricultural labourers at Mansfield. Attender of Sheffield Congregational chapels, never joining (Anderson, p. 29). Later often attended Quaker meetings and spoke at Brotherhoods (Fowler, p. 24). Wife ran Queen Street Congregational church's mothers' meeting for 17 years before moving to St James' Presbyterian Church, whose site she provided (*BDMBR* 3). Henry so admired R. W. Dale's *Laws of Christ for Common Life* that he reprinted some for circulation (Anderson, p. 30).

W. S. Fowler, *A Study in Radicalism and Dissent: The Life and Times of Henry Joseph Wilson, 1833-1914* (London, 1961). Mosa Anderson, *Henry Joseph Wilson: Fighter for Freedom, 1833-1914* (London, 1953). *ODNB* (mentioning Congregational transition to Quakerism). *BDMBR* 3 (JCGB). *WWW* 1897-1916. *WWBMP* 2. Papers at Sheffield University Library, Sheffield Central Library, Haverford College, and John Rylands University Library, Manchester.

JOSEPH HAVELOCK WILSON
16 Aug. 1859 - 16 Apr. 1929
MP (L-Lab) for Middlesbrough, 1892-1900, 1906 - Jan. 1910
MP (Coalition L) for South Shields, Oct. 1918-22

Seaman. Sunderland Boys' British School. Ran temperance hotel in Sunderland from 1884. Co-operated with Samuel Plimsoll in legislation relating to seamen. Founded National Amalgamated Sailors' and Firemen's Union (1887), which was reorganised as the National Sailors' and Firemen's Union, which in turn became National Union of Seamen in 1926, remaining president until death. On TUC parliamentary committee, 1890-98. Launched national seamen's strike, 1911. Secretary of Merchant Seamen's League. Unsuccessful candidate at Bristol, E, as Independent Labour, May 1892, standing against Sir J. D. Weston; Wandsworth, 1913, as Independent Labour; South Shields, 1922, as National Liberal. A founder of the National Democratic Party. Vocal supporter of First World War, and subsequently anti-socialist. Kept union out of General Strike, 1926. CBE, 1917. CH, 1922. Of St George's Hall, Westminster Bridge Road, London.

Thought to be Congregationalist (*CW*, 4 Jan. 1906, p. ii). But no religious claim found elsewhere.

J. H. Wilson, *My Stormy Voyage through Life* (London, 1925). *ODNB* (omitting religion). *WWW* 1929-1940. *WWBMP* 3. Papers at Labour History Archive and Study Centre, Manchester.

THE CONGREGATIONAL HISTORY SOCIETY

Secretary:
Rev C. Price
The Congregational Chapel
Pound Green
Guilden Morden
Royston
Hertfordshire
SG8 0JZ

Membership Secretary
Michael G. Mackintosh
The Flat
Trinity Chapel
St Matthew's Road
London
SW2 1NF

Treasurer
Rev Christopher Damp
Bunyan Meeting
Mill Street
Bedford
MK40 3EU

Editor:
Dr A. Argent
160 Green Lane
Morden
Surrey
SM4 6SR

Distribution:
Peter I. Young
125 Sudbourne Road
Brixton
London
SW2 5AF

Reviews Editor:
J. C. Morgan
19 Elia Street
Islington
London
N1 8DE